T0062879

The Golden Eagle of Father Sharip, Called Love, Democracy, Superposition

The Golden Eagle of Father Sharip, Called Love, Democracy, Superposition

Zamirbek Osorov

PARTRIDGE

To order additional copies of this book, contact
Toll Free 800 101 2657 (Singapore)
Toll Free 1 800 81 7340 (Malaysia)
orders.singapore@partridgepublishing.com

www.partridgepublishing.com/singapore

Contents

The Holy Grail of Democracy

Democracy looks for me as the best legacy of truly and great Love, as the eternal formula, Holy Grail which able alone to bless every dedicated person and society with the limitless power and marvel.

Preface

The history of the most successful soviet and post-soviet Kyrgyz family which casted light to the some great secrets on the base of happy, stable and healthy social environment and even revealed the enigmas of our nature and universe that needs to know for majority to catch up the blue bird of fortune and be happy and fruitful in any time, country and living situation and condition.

What does it really mean to be a good father? What is the legacy left Sharip aba for his children? Family values was a paramount importance for him.

The life of Sharip aba was a work of heart, soul and hand for benefits of his children, everyday's commitment and deals for the good of all. And he learned children working together not only for ourselves but for next generation too.

He stick to the point of absolute equality and justice on the relation with the sons and daughters and their own families.

As remembered his oldest son Kantoro Toktomamatov: "We would not have known beforehand that all basic recommendations and way of making deals with close relatives and our environment inherited from our father would be so valuable. So repeatedly and thoroughly compatible with the late opening new era and its unfolding propositions, that bringing utterly new possibilities and ways for gradually move ahead, step by step toward the unknown horizons and perspectives."

Why was that happening? Because this man knew something that hidden from general public and majority but what about going to better understanding some greatest minds and scientists in late decades. The answer is simple – the one who overwhelmed with love to his family and children, revealed the grace of democracy, rooted deep in our hearts and blessed by its power, influence and greatness and immortality and future welcomed him.

The dance of Sparticle it is the dance of quant of consciousness, these kind of quants alone in universe moved with limitless speed and instantly filled all breaches and gaps into our universe and defined it.

These sparticles are the firmament of our world, which created through dance of Democracy and Superposition, that's why our realm and dreams so deeply based on multiple choices and eternal love for the progressive realization a worthy ideal.

Sparticles of peace and prosperity

Please, dance with the democratic values
as often as possible,
play with them,
imitate and love
the countries with staunch and stable democratic institutions,
stick tightly to them,
entreating them to be with you or even cry out
if democracy don't understand you,
be strong and merciless with the any attempt and trend
toward dictatorship and violence
but be limitless merciful and careful with the democracy,
which often acted against herself,
if you want establish the real safety
and prosperity for your country and children
you must deeply respect and love this strange woman.
Don't believe for any other sort and kind of ideologies and state structure,
especially elude religious believers and claims and so called
founder of sovereign models of democracy,
which only camouflaged the most hideous and atrocious intend and content
of corruptive comrades, terrorists and bandits and maniacs.
Play with crystal-clear and marvelously pure and fresh
water of democracy
constantly reviving and refreshing
milk of honesty, justice and peace and prosperity.

Play with marvelous sparticles
going as deep as possible
to that mysterious game in family,
in love, in police
in local level
and in entire community and worldwide,
universe itself has born and grown with her dance and sparticles.

I

The phenomena of family institution

This book, dear readers, make you acquainted with the life of Sharip Jeenbekov, who was the founder of the very respected and prosperous family in modern Kyrgyz Republic. I personally knew the man, many met and talked with him and collected remembrances about him from various persons and his relatives. Having done that, penetrating to biography of this non-ordinary Kyrgyz aksakal[1] I intended to learn and unclutter the some secrets of our private and social life.

Americans well known widely for their appreciation and deep respect of family values. The same conclusion we may have when mentioned European and all other civilized nations – they are all abscessed with

---

[1]   Aksakal - old, wise man (from Kyrgyz language)

the strong passion to such things as good relation between husband and wife, between old and young family's members and so on.

In contrary to them among many families, belonged to the developed nations and countries, especially among the declined societies, we may have clearly observed as such vital values to get shrinking and crumbling or diminishing their power and role. It was a common practice for the Soviet empire what we called now as the broadly used way of systematic undermining, underestimating and downgrading the traditional family's values. Such spiritual vandalism was defined as the scientifically appropriated method of working of soviet totalitarian ideology, as the heart and soul of communist's propagandistic engine, which trying to tramp out, wiped and crashed down our national, cultural, historical heritages. And all that does in a favor of happy future of proletariats and workers, for the sake of some happy idyllic Red Atlántida, where supposed could to live in peace and prosperity the honest men, soldiers, pheasants after their total victory upon all enemies of working class. And where gradually created the some divine long-waiting garden and paradise of Mankind with marvelous fruits of Communism. Where vanished at all classes, casts and any other differences, the human diversities and unrepeated uniqueness, where all people had looking so simple, naive and lovely as illoes of Herbert Wells and where, of course, one night popping out from underground the morloks and goblins and starting to hunt and prey on them.

USSR had been a classical totalitarian state, which had overwhelming with the great ambitions and pretensions for world leadership and mercilessly suppressed such "trivial and bourgeois" atavisms like traditional family values. As a result within the 70 years of repressive experiments and hard works of red commissars, our leaders and political elite have very well learned and trained for the common practice of visceral despising traditional values, creating and nurturing in our soil the specific type of thoroughly ruthless and merciless staff, which late labeled wittingly as the homo-sovieticus, something or somebodies very like to personages and heroes of Orwell's "Animals farm".

It's quite understandable, why such kind of heavily, long-termed anti-family propaganda had coming out with so many problems in our everyday life. It's turn to be a common practice, when some or other soviet person that for the long-time working at states services, gained success and respect from Communist party and own comrades that nevertheless in his last years after retiring seriously failed privately, surrounded by ungrateful, odd and sometimes cruel family environment. When father suddenly discovered the ugly faces of grown children and the rapidly changed status of wife in the shadow of own misery and helplessness.

"Why you are all going to disrespect me now – exclaimed dolefully old comrade. – when I retired and need for your support and love?! I gave all my life to the Communist party, Lenin and Stalin and for yours better future – and doesn't such devotion deserve peace and respect from own children in his last days, why you are all grown so merciless and cruel toward yours father, yours bread-winner and supporter?"

Of course we are all desperately need to change our attitude to family and other traditional and basically values for preventing such tragedies and widening gap between generations in our society deeply traumatized by past cruel and unnatural experiences.

Maybe just here, in that ugly deformity of our family life, we can find the roots of so many imperfections, tensions in the attitude between young and old generations? We have accumulated in our soul and mentality the great masses of negative energies, which were the results and effects of our wrong past experiences and ideology that so strongly focused just on hate and confrontations with the free world.

As a result of such tragic misbalances and visceral antagonistic confrontation between social, ideological and family values, we have seen now so many failures and sufferings in our post-communistic society, so many frustrations among young and older, among brothers and sisters that unavoidable going to mutual disrespect, frigidity, to the weakness and fragility of society and state!

Admittedly all our nowadays conflicts, wars and tensions, if we casting broad view to that tendencies of world politics, we concluded unavoidable - all these tragic things are the fatal augment from our ignorance and bad education in family, school, in some or other social environment.

Our technocratic society and traditional soviet and post-soviet common mindset does not prepared for support family values and truly respect them and all our update problems and long-termed and even eternal conflicts and clashes going out from our bad relation with our children, with our spouses.

Our future might be better only through creating better and higher standards for every family. It's merely alone way, leading us to prosperity and better future – to help our children and grandchildren inherited more of our strengths and less of our weakness.

If parents, husband and wife are going to express lack of respect and love to each other, often quarreled openly and expressed mutual disgrace and intolerance – such action and behavior deeply hurt peace and safety in family. Children growing in such circumstances would inherit correspondingly instability, nervousness and lack of respect and gratitude toward each other and parents.

Why some sons and daughters have steadfastly undermined all attempts and long-termed efforts and achievements of their parents, which they did in favor of creating strong and healthy prosperous family?

Because they were not learned primarily to be a more tolerable and respectful to each other. Fathers and mothers possible gave them a good education and helped to find a good job, but they could not made their children to be a warm and kind between themselves and which may have fatal consequences for their future.

The lack of love, warmness, honesty, respect and sagacity in family relations that is the key factor which hindered communication and downgraded all attempts for creating a good attitudes between parents and children.

However, all these complex things in their harmony do get into family and blossomed there successfully just with the only way, most natural and fruitful, through implanting democracy principles.

So repulsing the democracy principles and propagate the ideology of hate and irretrievable fight with the basic human values, labelling them as bourgeois, eventually harmed our family, the source foundation of our society. It happened unavoidable because the democracy is the essential part of our nature. If we have trouble with it, disrespected its laws and principles, we have trouble with society, family, future, with the entire universe.

Let's keep to the point that way of vibration of the tinniest particles inside the atoms, according by Superstring theory, has determined the whole structure of our universe: it's basically physical capacities, gravitation and other forces, constants, dimensions and measures. In other words, what we are and where we born and lived, all our past and future experiences – absolutely all in our world depended from these vibrations.

The set of laws and states rules, fixed in our mindset and Constitution might be compared with the same particles and their unique vibrations, which determined the structure, nature and qualities of some or other societies.

Lack of love, honesty and harmony produced what we called as an authoritarian shape of mindset, defying by the vibration of lower frequencies of tinniest particles. That go on to produce so consistent and specific reality well known to humanity as type of state based on respect and rule of governing class or selected part of society, family, clan and so on. It is going to unavoidable to collateral social obscurity and suppression of personal undertaking and self-realization and even for totally enslavery of majority and individuals.

And vice-verse, the truly love has originated and settled here and everywhere the harmoniously and massively vibration of highest frequencies which produced and reproduced the basic principles, laws and values of Democracy in micro and macro levels of society and that has inevitable gone to rapid changings, to major and minor reforms which gradually leading to prosperity through unremittingly increasing ways and means for self-realization and social welfare and stability.

Sharip aba it seems knew the great truth of our existence and universe that Love is Democracy.

Democracy is the eternal choice, superposition of better intentions, the multitude of ways – and collapse for one path and step and again limitless possibilities and stupefying odd of great choices this is a deep patterns and witnesses of the great love and energy, sources and promises.

That's why happy and blessed the countries and nations those lieders, elders and government bodies deeply respected and even worshiped the principles of Democracy, because they worked, lived and acted according with laws of nature and universe. Consequently unhappy and destined to live in misery those states whose lieders misunderstand, despise or even artfully distort and derail this values for the sake of outdated traditions or personal enormous privileges and luxuries.

In certain degree, all the modern and past time totalitarian presidents remained or looked like an unfaithful and incompetent parenthood, who could not provide equality and justice in the relations among various sons and daughters and other close and far relatives into great family called state. Such parents and presidents have had a small number of dear ones, the highly privileged elite - and great number of neglected majority, substantial part of which lived in poverty and had a little chance to get up.

But even into bosom of unjust and cruel society, among some separated and long-term suffered families might be rested peace and prosperity and better hopes for future, for growing generation. If the parents beginning guide and make own family duties by the love and democracy, if they having create the climate of truly justice, mutual respect and prosperity.

You understood now why the parents who neglected by their obligations in family or wrongly carried them with the lack of love and respect toward future, unavoidable would be beaten tomorrow. The same truly upon presidents of states who despised democracy principles and hated them, soon or late these gentlemen when they lost power, retired or dismissed by the revolted children, they going to get into hard truth of our life and universe that only love and democracy are the most precious things that might to help avoid so many mistakes, traps and conflicts in every family and society.

Alas, many fathers and presidents too late got it, when they not have any chances for mercy and love from own children grown in fatal negligence, ignorance and lack of love in time.

In the same time sons and daughters, that gradually growing up and going to better understand parents, gradually accumulated awareness about how many efforts, energies, times and love invested to children their dads and moms, how powerless and humble might be their beginning without parental guide and care.

Of course, our life is a constant fighting for better future and more safely and comfortable environment for ourselves and our children and grandchildren. In addition, these aims have demanded many works and diligence - works in soul, mind and family, in local communities and states level. And again only democracy is widely opened gate, which not to bringing us or forced to better and fantastic future right now in one instance but show to us the way for the gradually changings and improving all sides and aspects of our world through our own increasing long-termed efforts and works.

Our first rate business and mission of our life

Many people asked him "what would drew you and motivated for such enormous, long-termed efforts and spending so much time, energy and other resources for your children?

Sharip Jeenbekov answered them, that he look for such kind of families obligates not just as for his father's duty only, but as for the matter of his personal self-realization, as for the prolonging, proceeding his life, activities and personality through children.

"That's why I turn my attention primarily to the creating good, sincere and warm relation in my family, as between children and parents, so between children themselves and also - what exceptionally valuable – keep good attitude between me and my wife. If your sincerely respected and loved each other and not shown themselves negatively before the children – it has had a great positive effect for future of yours growing generations.

In generally the most parts of our worries and problems just go out from the window if we learned together deal with and solved them.

Of course, we cannot avoid all painful problems at all, sometimes we must encounter with the very regretful challenges but we must tamed to do it diligently with the cold blood, holding tightly our emotions and trough consultations and advises, coming to conclusion that satisfied all sides.

Having reached the aims, I tried to give my children good education in family, in our local community of close relatives and outside of them - at schools and institutions.

Good education and love to knowledge, learning - these qualities and capacities are given us another key factors which helped to reaching the family prosperity.

If we look carefully around us, we observed that the most parts of our temporal crisis's, stressful situations in family, society or in government level - all such troubles-bearing things have happened just from lack of good education and competence.

Angry, envy, jealous, fears and others similar components of bad and negative behavior when you just waiting for confrontation with yours environment – all these negative features originated from bad or imperfect lessons taken in family, school and other social institutions".

The miracle of love and Democracy

Remember, when we loved sincerely somebody
more than ourselves,
we were all going to be look as truly Democrat,
who marvelously transformed and refreshed
and inspired by the great power of love.
We not only stopped to plan and do wrong things -
we even expelled totally such things from mind and soul,
and really able to do something extraordinarily,
something heroically,
ready for sacrifice ourselves
for the benefits of dear one.

Thus the magic of love, Democracy and truly greatness
go on above egoism and autocracy,
when person forget totally about own priorities.
So when every human society
and every member of it
learned to love and respect each other and all of them
with the same degree and responsibility
which well known for those who loved -
the democracy institutions
starting make up a wonderful miracles
in our reality,
unraveling all their hidden Quantum potencies and powers.

Sharip and Samara in the popular soviet resort of Kislovodsk, 1975

The equal investment in all children

That is a subject for what I turned my attention especially. Parents must be invest more love, energy and time to their children and do that equally, keeping good attitude with all of them. It is going to be especially valuable when yours children growing and starting one by one to create own families, when you encountering with the son-in-love or daughter-in-love or both of them and late with the growing number of children from your own children.

Keeping harmony and justice in that unfolding sequence and growing family tree I thought is a key factor for properly planting the seeds of our prosperity in future. If we have looked to our family as for the small society, containing various persons in various level of self-realization, every one of which might be happy and satisfied only if have seen and felt the continuous move ahead. Inequality, lack of respect and love are the most destructive things in the "family business."

Sharip and Samara surrounding by sons, daughters and grandchildren.

The firmament of great Love

For any honest, smart and well informed person
it's going to be clear in matured years
that Democracy is an authentic expression
of truly love and wise intentions
of great and kind intellect
toward any individual, society and Mankind,
which able alone to bring something extra-valuable
for long-termed sustaining life, prosperity and peace
in their great diversities and growing.
And the scientifically proven fact
that some key elements of Democracy
have created and existed primarily in our Universe
in fundamental law of Quantum Physic
witnessed about out Creator much more
than all ancient holy scriptures.

The 9 Kiev's cakes from Moscow were bringing to Kara-Kulja

More certain things you have to do, more you will rewarded. Better to do something sensible and touchable from big heart's effort and great diligence, respect, equality and love, than just to tell about such precious things. Literally, the true love, justice and other highest democracy principles, standards and laws installed deeply in every human being.

Sharip has sincerely respect for those, who will answered and granted him with the same respect tomorrow. But in pure love and respect of grandparents to grandchildren we have found out the same essence of pure love, respect and justice which might be call as democracy values.

The vibration of love

"I only exist into your dream. Literally, the dream reality exists inside vibrating atoms at the nucleus..." Tila Tequila.

That's why love is primarily, immortal and fundamental thing and exists everywhere and pervaded everything. In whole accordance with the law of Quantum Physic.

Once when father Sharip is returning from Moscow after business trip, he very astounded their colleges who have travelled with him, holding in hands 9 kiev's cakes[2] in paper boxes which were piled up one by one and tied as one heavy and tall structure.

---

2   Kiev's cake - the famous cake that was very popular in USSR as the best among other sweet deserts.

When he boarded to airplane prepared to fly toward Kyrgyzstan, he brings these cakes as handbag and asked stewardesses put it to onboard refrigerators.

His friends and colleges, some of them were heavily drunk, thoroughly poked fan on him for such strong attraction to the children. "Why you would not bay one or two cakes for all of them? You have feeling now and within a long journey to home much more comfortable, haven't you?[3] And think about - after arriving to Osh[4], how long you must drive by taxi up to mountainous Kara-Kulja? It is 3 hours of taxi driving! Just imagine what might happen with these sweets staffs in the road?

But father Sharip had been very convincing and stubborn to his love to his grown children and keep firmly and adamantly the sense and principles of equal rights, had bringing for every one of them the Kiev's delicious cake.

Of course, this man and father could made his private "male business" in Moscow after successful finishing his deal, gone to restaurants, night clubs, spent money for prostitutes as done it many generations of our visitors to Moscow. Instead, to be involved to all these adventures he bought the 9 Kiev's cakes and returned with them to his big family.

And he have done such thing all his life, lived and worked with the love and respect his family, wife and children.

No wonder that his family so flourished now and lived in prosperity and happiness, because every member shared own cake brought by Sharip father.

---

[3] The distance between Moscow and Kyrgyzstan is more than 3000 kilometers, air traveler spent on board nearly 5 hours.

[4] Osh – the second largest town of Kyrgyz Republic, called as south capital with the population reached 400 thousands.

When man deeply submerged to his duty with utterly passion, he make a way, leading to the unavoidable success. It's look as a scientist's commitment, when man day by night abscessed by the seeking answer for some theoretical preposition and question and eventually find it, after deepening and broadening substantially his knowledge, quality and competence.

Why Sharip aba was so successful as the father of big family? Because he had deep passion for these deal, duty and obligations. He really loved and adored his offsprings and was a wise man.

Seeing the world anew, as if it were new, is as old as our life. It's what all painters are trying to do, to see what's there, to see it in a way that renews it. It becomes more and more urgent as the reality gets worn flat and damaged, moving close and close to the total distraction. It becomes harder and harder to be honest and original, to be scrawled down on, to see things with an innocent eye. Innocence is much tied up with it. As the life gets progressively less innocent, you need a more innocent eye to see it. Yes, Martin Amis is right but it seems some people like Sharip aba will able not only seeing this world with innocence way but also acting with innocence way and create innocence reality.

And I do learned from him and bring to my people and readers my own 9 cakes. These are the special relishes for our nation as total independence, unconditional freedom, the strong society institutions in Kyrgyzstan, close attachment to the West's leading democratic nations and well balanced relations with all global powers, friendly and healthy tying up with the all neighbors as one of the central platform and green oasis right in the middle of Silk Road.

This is of course the stepping-stones of the path of our greatness as said David Cameron.

All these complex thing will not letting our nation to be defined as the state completely and utterly independent from Russia and make help us go ahead whatever we believe in and wonderfully transformed our state and nation.

If we have done all with right way, our world now not suffered so heavily from unprecedented scale of problems and not going down to total destruction. And UK instead of welcoming with the great honor the president of China, do the same things with our dear president of Kyrgyz Republic. Just imagine our lieder in golden cage with queen of England! And how Cameron invited our Atambaev to favorite local pub and they drink of beer and solving the migration crisis in EU and prime minister make a leverage on mighty Kyrgyz president to make a better deal with the lieders of Russia and China, totally depended from great Kyrgyz police. Alas, my friends, we are only with our geographical size slightly remained UK and still many people know nothing about our country. Of course, in other dimension and universe all the modern global gamers might look quite differently and you imagine that it is Kyrgyz Republic alone will able to save all our world from this stupendous and stupid falling.

The power of knowledge and experience of past's life

If I have not any other options,
except to be born in North Korea or Stalinist Russia,
of course, I will glad
again to live my early years in the great shade of dear comrades
and even gone through many harsh experiences
in my childhood and youth.
I will never complained
and be happy in any case,
because from my early days
in the shadow of our dear comrades
I trained and prepared
for escaping from this prison,
and could not stop me any doubts and propaganda.

Do you understand now, my friends,
why is that so cute to have perfect knowledge
about our present and past, traditions and history?

All our existent problems, dramas and tragedies,
beginning from bad governing and unperfected democracy, election system
and ending with repressions, tortures and genocides
of agonizing incompetence in power
many time happen in our history
which embraced thousands years.
However, for such long time
we had not accumulated the best knowledge
in substantial quantity and quality
for have the cumulative effect of democracy.

The Golden Eagle of Father Sharip, Called Love, Democracy, Superposition

Until now we merely not chance for better education,
it seems too far from Central Asia
to reach out Oxford and Harvard,
but now we have Internet,
please, not make heaviest mistake again,
underestimating of truly knowledge, its great power and effect.

II

The genealogy of aksakal

Why we cannot survive without Democracy?

(From the top secret of Superposition)

Imagine the reality of distant future when people will have opportunities not only to live without any geographical borders and barriers and cultural and ethnical differences but without any time frame and space limiting – without any barriers at all.

You might choice any transcendences what you want, make programmed and reprogrammed yourself to live in any time of your life - when you was young but not experienced and what you have best opportunities to change your life, world and Karma or instead maybe you preferred to live when you was old and mature and able to make a great discovery and for wise decision, or maybe you selected the multiple variations of your life, or wanted to send yourself to distant past epoch or distant future of Mankind and settled there.

In any case more yours choice and life going to be better, richer and more limitless, more will be precise, strong demand for keeping moral code and Democracy principles - they are also tend to reached to their acme point of complete perfection, greatness and beauty in complete and marvelous environment of absolute freedom. What's more, Democracy is a key formula for surviving Universe and all of us in our limitless greatness and power there and in Superposition.

Even if you preferred closed yourself into Universe of Nutshell or vanished and hidden in atom, electron and even more - to find rest in the wing of sparticle where ended Plank constant, unweaving the deep secrets of Quantum reality – there are also you must be keep with the greatest precision and accuracy the rule of Democracy in its Superposition for your benefits, increasing and happiness, because Quantum world it's a state of pure Superposition and their limitless miracles.

Do you understand now that all around us and inside us - Multiverse and Quantum world - based on Democracy? The core sense and deepest secret of Superposition is Democracy. John Keats might to say Democracy is Superposition and Superposition is Democracy, you must to know that truth for being happy, prosperous, lucky and wise.

When all people understand it and appreciate as the greatest truth, *our Superposition and Universe will revealed and unfolded all their marvelous greatness, possibilities and miracles that "never heard and seen by human" and even imagined by genius.*

And visitors from far and advanced future in space and time who lived in Superposition and mastered it but those do not deal with us because they are also submitted the principles and laws of Democracy and respected our choice even if its consequences are very limited and narrow, *they have respected our vast and disused empty Superposition as our legal cosmic right and property.*

And once more they were not entered to us hundred millions years before our origin, when our predecessors dinosaurs rumbled on Earth, because they respected our wild and unavoidable past before our origin and defying as human being.

Bur now, when we reached to the so high level we must act and think very carefully, greatly respecting Democracy, because human being and civilization could not survive without Democracy as they have not any chance for future without access to Superposition.

Sharip aba was born at 1928 in blessed autumn season, as he said himself, in the village called Biymyrza. This village today completely absorbed by town Kara-Kulja, compounding its basic part. It was a land of Sharip's forefathers – all seven generation and far more of them had lived here and buried in that valley. Sharip originated from Kyrgyz tribe called Tenisbay. His grandfather was Jeenbek, who was born at 1894 in Biymyrza village. Tenisbay as the head of tribe had a three sons – Bulash, Jalantosh and youngest called Biymyrza. Namely this youngest offspring of tribe head in the beginning of XIX century had come to Kara-Kulja valley and settled there.

Speaking generally Tenisbay is the widely distributed throughout of Kyrgyzstan and famous tribe as every one of other Kyrgyz 40 tribes. From the old times, this tribe has many rich and respected persons, datkas[5], mudarists[6], and just the wise men. For confirmation this strong notion we bring here just one example. Kasymaly Jantoshev, the great Kyrgyz historian writer who lived and created at first part of XX century and widely famous as master and founder of modern Kyrgyz prose and literally language, belonged the same Tenisbay tribe.

Jeenbek had not been a very rich man, but he was a person with property and dignity, very peaceful and tolerable, immersed deeply

---

[5]   Datka - semi-militarily, semi-administrative high title in Central Asia. "The Kyrgyz queen" Kurmanjan had such a title, widely known as Kurmanjan-datka.

[6]   Mudarist – the religious teacher, who educated in midrace.

into religious values, but to the traditionally Kyrgyz form of relatively free and mild Islam.

After October revolution when situation in country and most part of Eurasia dramatically changed, Jeenbek did not involve by the new tide, not stand as the part of new leading staff, called themselves as the red commissars, active lieders and their supporters but left as the very influential and respected local man. He kept himself at the distance as from enemies of new government so from the brainwashed communist's bigots. It's need to say such qualities as prudence, personal insight, sagacity, wisdom and good relation with environment have looked as family tradition and legacy which carefully protecting and sending from one generation to others in that dynasty of son of Biymyrza.

In whatever time and epoch they may have lived, what kind of tests may have met during their lifetime – the sons of Biymyrza in any cases got in peace, enjoying with relative comfort and stability within surrounding close and wide environments, keeping ancestral pride and dignity, respected in traditional society for their foreseen, tolerance and put in. And all of them avoided quarrels and conflicts as with the close relates at the inner circle, so with the neighbors or somebody also from outer circle, trying all rising problems and possible tension to solve out constructively and peacefully.

It must said beforehand about such features of this tribe and family mentality for better understanding biography of success of Sharip aba.

We have seen lot of other families, and their experiences, some of them look like as if all their seven predecessors were born and survived into hell, heaven sake, taped and trained there and eventually they pretty prepared and adapted for hellish style of life. They just cannot to live without quarrels, fights for trifles, without making great problem for nothing. That is, of course, utterly bad for society, when the substantial number of such persons, looking as risen from hell have lived around us, searching only the way for confrontation and contradiction and making our feeling worse and worse.

At the time of collectivization, one of the harsh economic-social experiments, which taken place in USSR in 30 years of XX century, Jeenbek cannot opposed to dishonest and cruel regime and its merciless force and power. He presented willfully all his livestock and other properties to the forming collective farm (kolkhoz) and himself had going to work in that kolchos as mere murap[7] At 1943 he was sent as soldier to the World War II, from where never returned at home and native land. No one know where and how he had killed and buried, it is known that he joined to the Unknown Soldier of WWII.

It worth taken mentioned here the mother of Sharip aba, Jeenbeks life-long wife and widow Ajar. She originated from Kyrgyz tribe called Kara Bargy. She was a very wise, kind and merciful woman. Her little brother Shermamat Pirnazarov also was recruited to WWII in 1944 years and not returned at home. Ajar had 18 babies, but only six of them survived - four boys and two girls. Others died in babyhood from starvation and other extremities and harsh tests of pre-war and wartime. The oldest son called Ermamat born at 1914 year, when he grew he is working as one of the chief of local organization of communist party, late appointed as the head of kolkhoz.

The next son of Ajar Toktokan, when he reached 27 years, was sent to WWII, where also killed. Toktokan survived three sons that lived, grown under the cure of Sharip and supported by him until married and made own families.

The firth son of Ajar Toktomamat was born in 1922. Many years worked as soviet local functionary, died in 1996. Sharip aba was forth survived son of Ajar, his little brother Suyunbay born at 1938 and in

---

[7]   Murap - man who responsible for water distribution in Kyrgyz villages.

1952 after finishing school died from heavy illness. His little sister Kaliman, born at 1942, was much luckier, she safely grown, married and survived ten children.

Ajar was born at 1894. Died reaching 63 year. She also originated from the good family; her father was a governor of local Kyrgyz community called as biy. "Her mother Surma - remembered Sharip aba - was exceptionally kind, clear minded beautiful person. My mother Ajar inherited her warmness and love – light and tender as a piece of cotton."

The grandfather of Sharip was a man called Pirnazar. He was alone son of his father and inherited his wealth and influence among people as a biy and son of biy. Shortly after October revolution in Russian and with the beginning civil war in entire Central Asia, he heavily hurt after falling from horse when he rode in mountain path, his animal was short by distant's pointed fire of gun belonged either a kozack or field chief of partisan or the agent of NKVD - its remained unknown still. He returned at home without horse and after some period of suffering from heart disease, died in jailoo Ajyke.

His father, the grand-grandfather of Sharip aba was man called Tanyryk. He was also had been simple and honest man who lived peacefully, not made even smallest harm for anybody around him.

His father - the grand-grand-grandfather of Sharip was Jaichibek. This man was respected person as a local aksakal and also well known as munushker[8] and saiapker[9].

The fifth father of Sharip was biy called Kojonazar.

---

[8] Munushker – the Kyrgyz that hunts to various wild animals with a trained eagle.

[9] Saiapker - hunter riding on horse with the hunting dogs

The sixth father - Biymyrza. He was along and amiable son of Tenisbay. The total number of sons and daughters of Tenisbay who lived now in Kara-Kulja closing to 2000 which consisted almost 20% of its population. There are also lived many offspring's of Bulash and Jalantosh, two older brothers of Tenisbay. These close related tribes have widely distributed throughout entire Kara-Kulja district and what's more, substantial part of them settled in surrounding villages and towns of Ozgon, Kara-Suu and Alay districts. By the way, part of Tenisbay tribe extended very far from Kara-Kulja - they lived in Yssyk-Kul valley of north region of Kyrgyzstan. The prominent Kyrgyz writer Kasymaly Jantoshev originated from this part of people of Tenisbay, who settled on the edge of "Kyrgyz sea"[10]. In his famous historical novel "Kanybek," Jantoshev depicted the colorful and multi-faceted life, behavior and traditions of Kara-Kulja and entire south region of Kyrgyzstan.

Now turning our focus from the head and founder of Tenisbay tribe to the Sharip aba and his biography.

He learned in one of primarily school of Kara-Kulja which bearing the name of Telman[11] until reached 5 grade and finished it but then the boy must be stopped education, because school building, very old-fashioned, deteriorated and ravaged, one day suddenly inflamed and burned out. It happened at 1942 years, when Sharip, 14 years boy was starting to work. His father and two older brothers are going to war; he left at home as the head of family.

---

[10] Yssyk-Kyl often called as Kyrgyz sea for its waste size and great depth, reached 700 meters below surface.

[11] According with soviet tradition many primarily and secondarily schools, cultural houses, art-studious, including formed collective farms (kolkhozes) and soviet farms (sovkhoses) that newly built and opened throughout entire country called officially by the names of famous revolution and communist lieders – international and local – in the honor and respect of their activities.

What kind of work he did not perform in these early years of his biography, where he was not been involved and committed! Within two years since he stopped his education, he helped to harrowing plowed field, assisted on grazing livestock, worked as scorekeeper, counter, register, weigher of kolkhoz's kirman.[12] Shortly saying he did all works in his commune, gone from many hard lessons and tests and learned many things and gradually accumulate awareness and what people said as knowledge of life.

The war years of Sharip remained the biography of thousands representatives of our old generation, whose young years put to that tragic and extremely hard period of our history. Many of our predecessors in their remembrances about that time, revealed the identical stories, how they at first going to work and where they worked.

We may have very well informed about this generation and its hard time, how it grew and shaped and what kind of life they lived for and what about dreamed, if we read the next books of our prominent writer Chingiz Aitmatov called "Samanchynyn joly" (A trail of heavenly mower), "Jamila", "Gulsarat."

At august, 1944, Sharip as smart and clever boy had sent by kolkhoz activists to oblast center Osh for graduating in so called Studying Combinat - a special form of learning center for preparation of various entry-level professionals – for the 6 month course of accountant.

---

[12] Kirman – the field storehouse where kolkhoz workers have collected various agriculture production (wheat, cotton and so on) going through the first stage of assessment, weighting and prepared for transportation to the big agriculture plants. Some kirmans were equipped additionally with the common kitchen, room for eating, resting place and other conveniences and commodities for working people.

"I am very happy, - remembered Sharip aba, - grateful and thankful to all, who sent me to that Studying Combinat (Uchcombinat), for this 6 month of learning. It was a crucially important 6 month for boy coming from mountain village, its turning to me as 6 years. Late I had graduated in much more solid institution and university but I have ever appreciated and valued this my first educational experience, which was exceptionally valuable and dearer for me.

He can make great jump here and he done it and future open its door more broadly for him. He was one of the first young man from Kara-Kulja mountains remotest district who got out there, studied and settled late down in such towns as Kara-Suu, Ozgon, Osh.

"It's need to say that people who lived and worked in that time were remarkably good, honest and responsible in their activities and duties. I know about it thank for Nurmamat Aidarov and Kunduz Syidanbaeva (the both were head of our kolkhoz) who sent me to study, prepared for long journey and late assisted me. Also I had warm memories about my teachers, how they received us, boys from remotest villages, created relatively good condition for life in big town and instilled us to gain knowledge, for deep digging in selected braches of it. The director of Combinat was Konovalov who lead the course for effective managing farms and various other activities. I was also warmly remembered with gratitude our tatars teachers – Gazizov (with the wife, also teacher) and Muchamadov[13]".

At 1945, after finishing study in Uchcombinat Sharip Jeenbekov returned to Kara-Kulja and started working as brigadier in kolkhoz. The next year he has been appointed as accountant of kolkhoz and worked on its job until 1953. Then he appointed as the chief accountant of

---

[13]   Tatars teachers - after October revolution in Central Asia with the educational mission had been sent many teachers and well educated persons from Tatarstan, the region of Russia, inhabited by Tatars, Turkic people who able easily understand Kyrgyz and others Central Asian nations.

veterinary hospital of Kara-Kulja district. Then since 1956 going to work as chief accountant of one of Kara-Kulja district division until 1961 year. At 1954 he starting to study in evening school on the base of opened secondary school which taken name of Stalin, and ended it at 1956.

At 1957 Sharip Jeenbekov moved to Bishkek for studying in financial-economical institution, which successfully ended in 1961. Within that time he also was been received to membership of Communist party of USSR.

After graduating, he sent as the communist party activist and chief of party committee (shortly partcom), to the kolkhoz of Telman, Kara-Kulja district. Next year he was appointed as the head of same kolkhoz and worked there until 1964.

At 1964 he was appointed as head of so called Consumers Union[14] (kerek-jarak koomu or Potrebsous) of Kara-Kulja district.

"The lieders of Kara-Kulja district asked me to work on this sphere, - remembered Sharip aba. – Honestly say, it was hard to me to receive such suggestion. How I can work if I do not know the matter, not prepared? But they said me, you are able to work, you well educated and then people respected you".

Since that time all his life and working biography will close related with the soviet trade system, and unexpectedly he come into his own, when had changing administering work as a head of kolkhoz to the activities relaying on the soviet trader system.

In the same time, for being prepare better for such kind of works he externally going to study in Bishkek agricultural university on department of economics.

---

[14]   Consumers Union – the state's organization of soviet system of distributions various products and items.

We are all engaged and tightly ties to each other's. We are all like one big family. You could not have known that all yours life, yours friends, relatives, yours environment have had waiting for you every day and every instant be the extraordinarily man and lieder, the best in your activities and decisions. How many souls, talents, stars, new beginnings and glorious ends will be strongly depended from yours possible success and self-realization!

When man have to had a strong and certain aim and strongly intended to be the best, it is going to be exceedingly impossible that he failed.

Nevertheless, there is we have some universal and very deep problem. We are rarely have seen as kind and good-hearted person transformed to the best lieder. Usually the bad guys and wicked ones occupied this top positions, when good and mild others left outside as daydreamers.

So Sharip aba show to us the way how to thinking, planning and acting exactly and correctly in your life if you want to gain success and the same time left as good person and excellent father.

If we are going with that way - all the simple and honest, ordinarily looking persons with the strong parental obligations and moral duties, of course, we not only realized ourselves in full measure but also - what exceptionally important - closed door for some really horrible and awful self-realizations when – woe for world and people! - evil genius and wrong ones get to chance for maximum unfoldment.

When a despotic rule has reigned whether in family or in society, it goes on to progressively worsening and terrifying things for every members in family and society and state, except one person in top of power maybe. The whole society and family coerced into deep and thick long-termed silence as a helpless and hopeful lambs. That's what I am so hating this system and practice, which suppressed and went down the human souls and lives.

The phenomena of evil genius

Of course, Stalin, Lenin, Fidel Castro and almost all dictators and bad guys in our history were been genius. You might labelled them as bad and evil genius and separated them from other kind of outstanding persons who reached to success without mass murders and violence, but that was not change matter. They had created our history until the rest plying with dreams and fantasies.

About Stalin's accuracy, diligence and great management skill *witnessed many historical facts. I bring here one of them - how he instructed his assistance to keep order in his new library – to put 5 thousand various books in right place and order, dividing on science, fiction, non-fiction, historical and philosophical directories. And into the every directory he suggests own carefully orders, according with value and importance some or other books. So the books have placed in his library in perfect orders and he fast reached to the searching items, when he wanted to do that.*

No wonder that this monstrous comrade so sticking to the right system in his work and duties will able so quick transformed from democrat to the one of the cruelest dictators and man of action in history of Mankind.

It is notable, that such things happened in the great country, which long ago suffered from traditional negligence and sloth.

As far as our society and people have to be trapping and suffering from apathy, indifference, conformity and very little worried about self-protection and protect future against "the evil genius" in power, of course, such comrades will be returned into our life again with the iron logic and fist of dictatorship repeatedly and diversified, producing the next round of cruel experiences.

The tipping point of success

As we have seen and make a point from my writing Sharip Jeenbekov very liked to study and never lost any chances for make up next step in his knowledge gaining activities.

"You must many work and learn if you will wanted to be less depended from others and lived more free, prosperous and lucky". His children Sharip also was educated and learned well and prepared them to be diligent and greedy for gaining knowledge.

In his working practice as the head of Consumers union of Kara-Kulja district. Sharip Jeenbekov one of the first in Kyrgyzstan used a new, progressively method of trade with the consumers goods. Instead of keeping predominant part of various items in storages and sometimes going to practice of selling out part of them in shadow, he turn to trade with open way, when all the goods spread out on the shelves of shops and buyers have to had free access to inside them for carefully selecting what they wanted, before deciding to bay or not it. Also for all deals with customers had been used the transparent cash registers equipment which helped preventing "black money circulation" throughout all dozens shops, trade centers, markets and other facilities maintaining into the district area.

As a result of such innovation in practice of Soviet extremely rigid and primitive system of local trade, the commerce turnover within Kara-Kulja district grow up to 30-40 percentages, which had a positive impact for economic dates of the sub-region, which included Kurshab, Ozgon and Kara-Kulja districts.

Eventually, when Myktaly Amanov, the head of Kyrgyz Republic Consumers Union come to the south of Kyrgyzstan with the inspection visit, he carefully observed how functioned refreshing and reshaping trade infrastructure of Kara-Kulja district and was very satisfied with such innovation and diligence of Sharip Jeenbekov. Its need to say that such achievement into one district was very sharply contrasted with the deep stagnation in that sub-region, where Amanov during that visit surfaced many defects, imperfectness, lack of innovation and confidence and enthusiasm - and decided to change the head of Ozgon Consumed Union Vorornenko for the negligence and indifference, shown on his duty. He recommended Sharip Jeenbekov on his place and turned with such suggestion to the head of Communist party of Ozgon distict Arstanbek Duysheev.

Duysheev answered that he agree with such suggestion, but this matter must been additionally overlooking on higher oblast committee of communist party.

In that time, Akmatbek Suyunbaev headed the communist party's organization of Osh oblast, which covered entire south region of Kyrgyzstan.

Muktaly Amanov told to Akmatbek Suyunbaev about Sharip Jeenbekov as for the good and promising manager and recommended him for appointment as the new head of Ozgon district's Consumers Union.

At first Suyunbaev objected, saying that against this candidate we have critical letters and complains from local people.

Amanov had parried to him, if people sent critical letters in his address then it needs to investigate the contents and reasons of these writings and we know the truth. I am himself inspected the area where worked this man and convinced that we have deal with the good manager. If we not supporting such staff then our works barely go ahead.

Honestly say, many local people criticized the activities of Sharip Jeenbekov, but it was mainly the planned actions from the other competitors who also claimed for leading position, but having little chances for winning compare with Sharip, trying compensate own lack with the enormous efforts to blackmail him, create negative image, distributing anonymously written letters and complaints for his account to various states bodies. However, in that time all their attempt failed, because Amanov personally involved to the matter and come to the right conclusion.

Since that time Sharip Jeenbekov worked with Muktaly Amanov 18 years. He remembered his chief with great honor and respect, telling about him as "for very honest and decent person with the high human qualities and energies".

Sharip aba worked as head of largest in Kyrgyzstan Ozgon district's consumer union until the 1977 year, in that time substantially supported and increased local infrastructure, rising number of trade shops and distributive-selling check-points throughout entire district up to 400 units. It was a great leap ahead in the matter of creating modern trade system in mountain and remotest part of Kyrgyz Republic, maintaining new facilities, producing hundredth new jobs and providing better social service for local population. We just mentioned there the several big realized projects like the Beer producing plant, the trade centers "Tynchtyk" and "Ubileiny," restaurant "Kara-Shoro" into Ozgon town, the procurement agencies (zagotkontory), warehouses for Kurshab and Ozgon agriculture sectors and farmers, the net of small shops along the main roads - all that objects and commodities built up under the top managing of Sharip Jeenbekov. And it was just the small part of works and projects carrying out in his time. At 1976 Sharip Jeenbekov for the great impact in social-economic development of Ozgon district had been awarded by the respected name of "Honored Worker of Trade of Kyrgyzstan."

-I'd like to be involved in various building activities, - said Sharip aba. – All my life I was busy with such works, which are very important, because every new deal begin from planning and building a new accommodation. For gain success in every undertaking at first, you must prepare good place and provide them with all desirable and needful conditions and then may have demanded a good work. If you cannot do that, you may have not reached your aims.

With the managers of soviet trade systems. Ozgon, 1972.

At 1981 year Sharip Jeenbekov was appointed as the head of Kara-Suu districts consumers union, it was also the biggest district in Kyrgyzstan with the large trade infrastructure and great possibilities.

He worked here 6 years and for that span of time thank for his activities Kara-Suu towns and district's trade facilities renewed and modernized substantially. There were been built and going to make services the trade complex "Kubanych", book selling center "Kitep Uyu" (The house of books), supermarket "Ay-Suluu", district's restorant and great number of others new facilities, shops, distributive points in every corner of district, which not only helped improving buseness activities in that famous town and densely populated region but also made a better their outward fashion and architecture.

At 1986 Sharip Jeenbekov will sent as the head of Kara-Kulju district's consumers union. Of course, he immediately had to plan and start several exceptionally valuable infrastructural projects over where like modern Trade center.

For the short time, inhabitants of that remotest mountain district had been benefited with the next facilities:

1. Kara-Kulja Covered market,
2. Modern bread making factory, with the daily capacity to produce 20 tons freshly baked bread,
3. Animal market.

In addition to, in various part of Kara-Kulja district had been built up and equipped 12 small shops and trading point, preparing for selling various items, this distributive system, as said local people, will able to operate 100 years. There also built and given for active use electro mill, with the daily capacity for producing 5 tons of flour, oil producing plant, rice cleaning plant, lorry cars repairing enterprise and many other similar soviet–style facilities and utilities so needful for local economy activities and supporting the body of socialist planning economy.

Especially the bread making factory which was equipped by a modern technology and Kura-Kulja's crown jewel the Covered market have made substantial impact to the social-economic development of this remote mountain district, for reviving local trade and other business activities and growing welfare of population. In addition to these new buildings, which taken place in the center of town, thank for their architectural values and merits have refreshed and reshaped the whole image of Kara-Kulja.

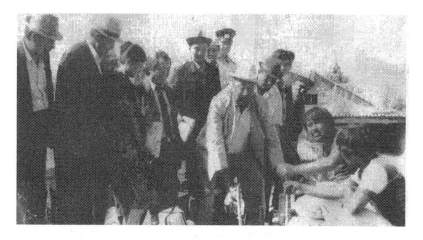

Lying the first symbolic stone to the ground of the new
trade center, going to build in Kara-Kulja. 1993.

Within 10 years, when Sharip Jeenbekov had worked as head of
Kara-Kulja district provisional union there were realized many such
infrastructural projects, which not only improved economic and better
prepared people for surviving but helped to look this small town more
update and attractive for living.

Considering the bread making factory, it will be not excessively to
mention its exceptional role during the tragic events in south of
Kyrgyzstan in summer 1990, when trade and other activities into the
entire region completely blocked for the month, this factory proceeding
to work unstoppable and provided karakuljiners with the freshly baked
cheap bread every morning.

Many locals believed that Sharip aba saved them, it's look as if he
anticipated the approaching in not so far future a harsh days and events
and knowing about, made a urgent preparation.

By the way, it is a main problem of many Kyrgyz districts, towns,
remote regions what we call as lack of infrastructural development - a
bad roads, bad accommodations, outdated technologies and so on.

Later many people and experts mentioned and made official reports about relatively good conditions and development of trade infrastructure of such south districts of Kyrgyz Republic like Kara-Suu, Ozgon amd Kara-Kulja. We not make a mistake if not only confirmed that evidently facts but also added that personal impact of Sharip Jeenbekov for improvement of all these districts and their assets were exceptionally valuable, irretrievable and unforceful.

Until today in many town and villages belonged to these three districts you can find lorry cars, trucks, mobile shops and others items which still actively used by local peoples, which had been privatized them – all these technics equipment's were been bought and installed at the time, when Sharip Jeenbekov worked as head of consumers unions.

He preferred to work hard and learn more rather than depending strongly on the government body or someone else like rich and influential persons, because if it happened, they might own your soul and bringing you and your future some risks and even threats.

Generally Sharip aba goes about his everyday's duties as for essential work for making everyone around him and in his family look and feel more better and prosperous by the times passing. Only the great and wise love will able to inspire such sort of diligence and activity.

And I am also inspired by this man, whose personality grown and shaped within the quite different times frame, wanting now strongly to do the same things and reached the same great success, using fruitfully all possibilities which unfolded upon us the modern reality with the marvel of internet, mobile phone, with the great achievement in social knowledge's, with the keen revelations of democracy and western values, with the magic brace of Quantum physics, cosmology, astronomy, the Unified field theory, Superposition, science of getting rich, art of visualizations and attractiveness.

As Sharip aba made a great impact for his family and surrounding people and to their future so do I trying now to get to every our readers and share with him what I found and discovered - and help to all of them to be fruitful, prosperous and blessed in their time.

Let not only our state and our citizens, but entire word opened the deep secrets of welfare, happiness and love.

Some brush-strokes to the portrait of Grace

The values and principles of Democracy in their Superpositional enfoldment together with Multiverse theory have given to us the most convincing and spectacular witnesses about Highest Intellect and its sacral activities, far stretching aims and plans. Having opening our insight to the truly nature of divinity before whom we stand and who possible created our World or managed and sustained all these grandeur evolutional processes in micro and macro level in its combining harmony and unity.

That absolute and stunning limitlessness and greatness around us and inside us, in the Universe which surrounded us and in the fundamental base of our reality that is going from the tinniest Quantum world and its weirdest laws and ending with Multiverse — all these wonderful things told us about the great love and Intellect, about the eternal Wisdom and Democracy.

Who else might to present us the beautiful and perfectly tuned world! Who else might to present us so great number of ways and possibilities opened before us one by one with the every our step! And when we made our choice as we wanted it, who else created such marvelous laws which taken such great care about us and our choices when we nothing lost, because set of all other multiple ways and choices, which was not used by us, saved and preserved in Multiverse?

We asked one life from our God but he presented to every one of us the multiple, limitless lives - instead one Zamir where existed limitless number other my doppelgangers. What a wonderful world!

Our Creator has shown the great, limitless respect for our choices on every instance of our existence, even if we going with wrong way, give us chance to see what happened late, in the same time keep safely our other realities and lives and not forget about sinners, and giving them chances for wholly recovery and reestablishment- and everywhere and forever keeping honesty, liberty, democracy.

Yes our world is the absolute Superposition of Love and Democracy, unavoidable leading to apotheosis and triumph of Love and Justice.

We are all born in perfect Love and Democracy and returned to perfect Love and Democracy.

The oldest son of Sharip Kantoro with spouse Meerim

III

The remembrances

Mamat Orozbaev,
ex-head of Consumers Union of Osh oblast, ex-deputy of Jogorky Kenesh (Kyrgyz Parliament):

-I know Sharip–ake since 1970 when I was worked as head of universal trade center in Jalal-Abad town, he then headed of Ozgon district's Consumers Union. Through Sharip-ake late I make a friendly attitude with the others members of his big family - with his wife Samara eje and his children. His oldest son Kantoro turn to be my close friend, with the next son Jusupbek also I have a good relation; he looks for me as my own little brother.

It's needless to say how the name of Sharip ake has respected in our region and the system of state's activity in the south of Kyrgyz Republic. He has some precious peculiarities in his mentality, which explained his stability and heavy weight of his every step and behavior. No matter what times, tests, sufferings or instead through blesses and honors of fate he goes on - he has kept the same shape and sense of honest and decent, welcomed man, deeply respected and appreciated by his friends, relatives, colleges and just by public and his native inhabitants and comrades. When he sat in very responsible chairs and has to make a serious decision according with high position, as a man he had been the same Sharip, open and accessible for friends, ready to warmly welcomed them. With the colleges and partners from state's works and governing structures he also keeps equal and long-termed attitudes and relations, even when some or other persons retired or lost their influential positions, he proceeds to support old connections and friendship – it is one of the best capacities of this old man which so contrasting in comparison with many other influential figures.

Among such his friends were been Duysheev, Japarov and others, Sharip ake had warmly welcomed them as his dear guests, when they were in top position at state services, and later, when they were retired, Sharip has kept the good attitude, invited them to Kara-Kulja and himself also visited to them, communicating with old friends and colleges heartily, remembering old days and supporting each other.

In his managing practice and working with staff Sharip Jeenbekov used method that late would be known as the system of incessantly leaning, he loved his work and spent many time and efforts for increasing competence in favor of better performing his duties. In work with his subordinate's staff, he tends to turn opinion at first for better capacities and qualities of every person and helping to launch and make progress on them. For that reason he systematically prepared and conducted learning's seminars and trainings for own personal, sending many of them to Bishkek, Tashkent, Moscow to improve their qualifications from the practices and everyday duties of the leading trading unions and organizations of USSR. And he was very polite and carefully when he makes deal with everyone. For the long time of working as the head of Consumers Unions in Ozgon, Kara-Suu, Kara-Kulja - no one from his staff have not had problem with the law, not broke rule, involved to corruption and charged by court.

And he could work remarkable fast and successfully for benefits of mere people and social-economic development of heading districts and towns! How many buildings left after him! Before his arriving to Jalal-Abad, the towns canning factory was an increasingly degraded and crumbled object. For the short time after his appointment as the head of this factory, he completely restored and modernized it. And how changed and renewed Kara-Suu for the 5 years working of Sharip-ake as the head of local Consumers Union!

About his great tolerance level and insight of his mind has clearly witnessed one event which had to happen between us.

At 1986 when I was the vice–head of Consumers Union of Kyrgyz Republic and Sharip-ake is going close to retiring age, when for him left only two years, I suggested him to change his place - to work as the head of Consumers Union of Kara-Kulja district, leaving his current position in Kara-Suu.

Of course, such exchange will not welcomed at first by Sharip ake, because Kara-Suu district was much large than Kara-Kulja and he clearly understood what he lost if we come to agree about this my statement. But I told him: "Sharip-ake, the day of your retire is closing and it needs for you as for manager with so great experience to work for the benefit of native district and yours people. There are - in Kara-Kulja – lot of works need to be done. Who also so fitted for that, except you and it high time to make something valuable for you native land?

Sharip ake answered me "I have got to think about your suggestion for a while. Give me a one week".

After week he come to me and told, you were right, Mamat, I am receiving your suggestion.

It was the happy instant for me too, I congratulated him and lifted personally on my office car to Kara-Kulja district and presented it for him. Life itself make a proof little late that such decision of Sharip aba was one of the best and wisest in his autobiography.

Since that time until 1995 he worked as head of Kara-Kulja district's Consumers Union, despite for his retiring age and his desire go to rest, we could not to find a proper man in his order too long and asked him to proceed his work. Within that span of time Kara-Kulja district completely renewed, as before it Kara-Suu district, enriched substantially with the many beautiful socio-economical objects, trade-centers, net of shops – these are just a few of the amazing transformations that have happened thanks for Sharip Leenbekov on the top of organization which had obliged for reviving local commerce activities and services.

Among the managers of soviet trade system, Moscow, 1980.

He is a man from nature granted with many good capacities and qualities - very rich and blessed human. Look to his sons, daughters, sons-in-law and daughters-in-law – they are all grown very friendly, polite and respectful in terms of attitude with parents, other relatives, neighbors or between each other's! It seems God itself created such brilliant unity and family! Sometimes I have to catch up myself being deeply jealous when I see such kind of family idyll. I hope and want that my own children have learned and imitated much good things from Sharip's example, when they growing, creating own families and relations with his offspring's. However, it is clear that we have deal with the exceptionally rarely appearance. Will we look the same just in heaven, I do not know – such kind of family phenomenon?

I have tried long to find answer for that mystery and coming to next conclusion. For my opinion, many things explained not only by Sharip's extraordinariness but also by his wife Samara's human exceptionality and sagacity. They both are very wise and leveled persons, foreseen and diligence and joined effect of this harmonious couple have to a great impact for their family advance, increasing prosperity and its promising future.

Jusupbek Jeenbekov,
ex-gubernator of Jalal-Abad oblast,
Preliminary and extraordinarily embassy of Kyrgyz Republic in Saud Arabia.

-For all of us our father appeared to be as someone like a holly man, really. He deserved forever for our deep respect and love through his warm attitude, love and respect to people with them he chanced to communicate or who just surrounded him. Our dad at first appreciated and deared in every man this kind of quality and himself belonged to that type of wise people which keeps very carefully a human relation.

I have clearly remembered as he told to us many time, until these words fixed in our mind: "My dear children, when you are walking outside, at first all people, who met with you, received you as human being. They do not know who are you, how you wise or rich, not familiar with your hidden values, with yours social position, achievements, prehistory and so on. Most people even do not like to know about such things. But all of them from the first instance turn opinion for you human capacities. That was a most important thing! Therefore, I have wished to all of you wherever you going or whenever it have been, at first keeping the good, welcoming, kind attitude with all people with them you encountering, make a deal or just meeting somewhere or sometime.

I am now myself grown man, father of two children and for many sides of family life starting to look differently than before than I was not been so experienced. And my deep respect and love to my father just grown with my own maturity.

My father never started any kind of deal in family or outside with how to say indifferent state… especially with irritation or despair. It seems that such things were been completely incompatible with his nature.

Once more, I never remembered that he had raised his voice for his children, even when they expressed themselves with evidently wrong way; he protected us from our babyhood from stressing us, psychical pressure and so on. Of course, he carefully guided and observed what happened at home and looked for our behavior and he certainly reprimanded for us if we done wrong things and punished us. But he had done it with own polite verbal, emotional way, carefully explaining the possible negative effects of our miscalculation if we stack on it. Similar behavioristic comeliness and perfectness have great impression for all of us, and we also trying to be in good attitude and mood with father, in any case we are all afraid to offend and injure our father even at smallest degree.

Asylbek Sharipov,
Ex-speaker of Jogorky Kenesh (Kyrgyz Parliament):

-For example, if one of us, his sons, goes wrong and feel guilty, father doesn't have to quick with angry reaction and punishment. If it happened before dinner or evening supper, he invited all to sit down around dastorkon[15] and have a meal in peace and comfort, and only after finishing it, father called to himself "the guilty person" and going ultimately face-to-face deal with, investigate the case and explained him where and why he lead himself incorrectly and what need for getting better. He never raised hand to us, even when we did frankly stupid things, and more we never heard from him the loudly shouting. It's always astounded and inspired me - our father's great willpower and endurance.

We have been trying to establish a good dialogue and good attitudes through it. It has should not been taken in negative sense. And we should someway, somehow to forgive each other's, may have to do that in attitude between close relatives and friends. We are all human beings and sometime done wrong things, showing negligence, lack of respect to someone near to us or making mistakes. So sticking point is to be a capable to get over it, not fixing on such things. That's I think is a very serious matter.

I am also trying to do the same things in my attitude with my own children, made himself as close to them as possible and expressed the same politeness even when life demanded from me to be a firm and show a firm parental obligations. I always remembered what my dad had done or imagined what he will said and how acted in such situation? And such things very helped me to find right way and right words for solving problems which sometimes arise in my own family.

When I filling myself happy and lucky even if that happened far from my children and family I have had a good habit in such airy instances - to wish in my heart for my relatives and dear ones the same happiness and raptures in their life. It's very simple... a sort of praying or mental

---

[15]   Dastorkon - traditionally Kyrgyz families having dinner, sitting on blankets around a special low dinner table, covered with the dastorkon (tablecloth) on its put prepared meals, breads, caps of tie and sweets.

exercise but it deeply grounds into our sub-conscientiousness with own positive effect to our life.

Jusupbek Jeenbekov:

-I wanted to keep my own children with the same principles and rules and attitudes but I am desperately filling lack of my personal confidence, tolerance toward my own offspring's, sometimes I caught myself that speaking with them on high frequencies or even crying to them. When my father heard about, he strictly criticized us, asked and demanded from us to be polite and warm with children. According with his strong belief the good relation between fathers and children, mutual respect have cemented from early days.

It always astonished me, from what kind of tests, sufferings and sacrifices went on our dear father until grown all of us and prepared for life - 11 his children, gave all of them the happy childhood, graduated according with interest of everyone, helped to create own families, built own homes! Compare with him I have only two children, but, nevertheless, cannot do the best in my deal with them, as could and did our father into the much more complicated situation.

Kantoro Toktomamatov,
rector of Jalal-Abad University of business and management

-Sometimes in our big family also has happened some frictions, tensions, dissatisfactions between some members. However, we know how deal with such things and minimize their detrimental impact in time, instead of mutual confrontation, going to make concession.

Our parents had given to us very good lessons and practices about such subjects. Father not only never told to us in raised voice, he did not like at all the notable speeches. He directed us, how to say it, with own attitude. We just merely afraid to hurt him, when we were young, and much late when we are all grown, we trying avoid it, even in slightest degree hurt him. Even when I spoke to him through phone calling, just from intonation of his voice I know what he thought about me, glad or regret to me and what I have to do or vice-verse not to do for being in good terms with him that he approve me and my behave.

Since our early days, he have never looked down to us, shown disrespect or forced us to do what not liked us. But he supported every our step and attempt to deal with the other people, make a good attitude with the surrounding neighbors, close and distant relates and of course, searching truly friends and after finding them, keep such person with right ways.

Father often said to us - never make suggestion about some or other people based on circulating gossips and rumors. Until you have seen all with own eyes, it is very difficult to make a truly conclusion about some or other man, his behave or event which happened with. That is why he avoided himself to do a sharp and quick suggestion and asked us to be a very careful on this account.

This is seemingly the alone road leading everyone toward the peace, prosperity and safety. Moreover, in the more broad scale, the same priorities need for the reaching peace and harmony in our society. Without mutual tolerance and readiness to forgive each other's and culture of making right agreement and coming to consensus, we cannot step ahead and we never have got to get out from crisis of mutual unfriendliness, hostility and lack of confidence.

Forget about all world's problems and international tensions between global and regional superpowers, for you much better will be to begin creating harmony and peace on your small community, lessening tension on your family between its members, sons and daughters! Try to do that, make a wonderful transformation at this primarily level. Find way for peaceful resolving all heavy conflicts between close relates, learn to respect and love parents, others relates, neighbors and maybe you better understand how create good attitude with own offspring's and future – yours children and grandchildren. If you could really make a success in that direction, you would not only build happy family and strong firmament for your welfare, it would be your best impact and contribution to the unity of Kyrgyzstan, for building its peace and prosperity.

Father with the sons. 1978.

God and Democracy

The truly Democrat-ruler is those who creates a system that works properly by itself, when people are going to forget who their president, ministers, mayors and so on. And these people are working better and better, made own choice and happiness and prosperity themselves. The system allowed it.

The true God if he had really existed and participated in creating this world seems to me as the fundamental source of Democracy in his great comeliness, this God not only created a perfect world and the laws that work properly without him, but hidden himself completely, so that no one has able to discover Him, nor calculate.

Why he did go for such trick?

Because he wants at first planted to the soul of human creature this kind of strange religion and belief that all nations have to believed and worshiped to Democracy, as to the truly and along God, and through such belief and action opening their own unlimited powers and resources for changing the world according with laws and principles of Democracy.

If God has shown himself openly, people going to believe more to his miracles than to Democracy. God put the principles of Democracy above themselves, behaving as the truly great democratic ruler.

Only the laws of Democracy can tell us about the true nature of God, who seems to be saying to all of us - no matter believe you to me or not and once more have I really exist or not - you have to make their own destiny and to be happy, increasing and strengthening Democracy.

That's why those who deeply respected and loved Democracy will respected and love God and Mankind and future and they shall be blessed from generation to generations as Abraham's sons who inherited the lands and great number of nations on Earth.

Begaly Tagaev,
PHD, Kyrgyz state University, author of monograph "Naziktik temasy Kyrgyz adabiatynda" -Tenderness as esthetic category and its expression in Kyrgyz literature in modern, old and ancient sources.

The law of tenderness

I come to conclusion that our world and humankind have to find way to harmony and peace just through keeping laws of justice and tenderness.

Yes, John Lennon and Leo Tolstoy are right, - we have to do all to escape hate and war and turn to love.

Moreover, every living creature in the world, every entity and any object, even among them the tiniest and insignificant as any phenomenon and manifestation of the objective and subjective world should be considered as unique and extraordinary things with reverent attitude, understanding and comprehension.

Than far forward move humanity, than clearer, deeper and more fully aware that one of the main obstacles to its development are the rudeness and sinicism which imposed by imperfection of its existence and past experience. And Sharip Jeenbekov, his life, works and achievements might be the best illustration for the theory that love and tenderness must be in the focus of Mankind, if we want to survive and create the happy future.

Arzymbek Osorov, ex-deputy of Kyrgyz Parliament in Soviet time, who elected 5 time to Jogorky Kenesh of Kyrgyz Republic since 1960 to 1985 years.

-In any case Sharip Jeenbekov is a lucky one. He waded through a lot of Soviet ideological and dogmatic rubbish correctly, in the time when business and marketing activities were been strictly banned he, nevertheless, done a right things, involving to work in trade area, in purely economic sphere and make a great advantages in old time when no one have any idea about marketing economy. Certainly when came time for transformation our society from command-administrative system he and his children have been better prepared for such steep changes in the life, again making a great success and advantages. He has got it, my old friend, better than anyone other.

Omurbubu Begaly, famous poets, philosopher, common lieder.

-Sharip aba was the epitome of lovely and wise father character that so few parents have. I did not know well this aksakal but I pretty well familiar with his oldest son Kantoro Toktomamatov, the rector of Jalal-Abad commercial university, who are good person really, clever manager and prominent expert in high educational sphere of Kyrgyz Republic.

Ashirkul Kurban kyzy, the contemporary of Sharip Jeenbekov, prominent gardener and housekeeper.

-What our Toktogul had in common with all other great talents, it is a keen interest to poetry and art of aitysh, improvisation. Whenever or wherever at his life time had happened something interesting and valuable as festivals where invited poets and announced planning competitions between famous akyns[16] or just emerged a new promising talent, Toktogul reached out there at first, delaying all other duties and obligations for the participating in competition or just hearing the improvisation of other poets and learning from them and honing own style and art.

He was a poet have to be the best, how telling about such sort of person Bo Yeson. He was really 90 % of his time spent for preparedness and 10% for performance, improvisation.

The similarly strategy, commitment and self-discipline we have seen in the life of some of our contemporaries like Sharip Jeenbekov, which manifested in own specific area –very common for majority and that is why so valuable and precious for all of us. He used to the same formula of spending 90% of his time and efforts for preparedness, practice to the 10% of performance. As a result he gradually mastered himself as a creator of big family and its long-standing prosperity, safety and success. He had not wanted that his kids fate sealed and done everything for their progressively increasing and happiness.

Lack of love

We are all prepared to stand trial before increasingly looming future which will used own scale of justice, honesty and wisdom. Only likes of Sharip aba, Margaret Thatcher, Abraham Lincoln can enter to the country, called future, have place into its marvelous garden where reigned empire of Democracy. No any dictator, rouges, perpetrators, corruption persons cannot enter here, because they were the enemies of future.
Love me tender asked us all universe if you wanted to live happy and prosperous and protected from all sides.

---

[16]   Akyn – Kyrgyz poet, used traditionally for nomads the oral art of creating poetry.

The Golden Eagle of Father Sharip, Called Love, Democracy, Superposition

The shortest novel about the grand evolutional story: "The little work with the great love"

Our world has overwhelmingly
need to love, not to war.
Look, how strong and powerful acted
the national lieder of Russia,
as a man of replicated lies and head of states of conflicts, plots, violence
and hatred.
Who can this fatal wrongness to stop
and the deep rooted evilness extract off?
Only great love to world, peace and Russian.

Look for the millions religious fundamentalists,
who ready with the name of God to kill innocent people
explode skyscrapers and get to down airplanes.
Who is taking to born this horde of murders and killers?

Only lack of love
to the dodged mass who lived in the deserts, bearing underground
sea of gas and oil.
Their land so rich astronomically
but also so dangerous catastrophically
due to lack inwardly and outwardly
of truly freedom, hope and love
for unhappy mass trapped in prison of hate and bigotry.

IV

About Kyrgyz regionalism and tribalism

We are all have trapped by bloods of Kings

We are the nation that originated directly from the prominent sons of great kings and heads of ancient dynasties and that is make us so unhappy and produced so many our major problems and rooted so many our fatal weaknesses.

We have born to rule by others, even if these others smarter than we, we loved to look as the others worked for our benefits.

Few of us experienced to work personally, undertaking something new, expressing creativity, but many of us very skillful for steal and rob of what belonged others.

Few of us predisposed for strenuous, severely efforts to make something valuable but lot of us predisposed for stagnation, leisure, melancholies and others aristocratic diseases.

It's very hard to make business and create good environment for performing various activities in country, inhabited thoroughly by offspring's of great kings, sultans, emperors, kagans and others highest elite of world history.

Just imagine how you feeling personally if you would surrounded by successors and co-successors of Alexander the Great, Kudzulla Kadfis, Attila, Chingiz chan, Tamerlan, Babur, Suleiman, the husband of very beautiful Hurrem and others kings of kings, who governed by all states and continents. Many of us still got a sick from ancestors' enormous activities in past centuries and millenniums. The blood of every Kyrgyz boiled and energized incessantly from the supra-active genes of founders of German, Russian, China, Hindu, Japan empires!

Who would be able for good work in such preconditions and such badly hierarchy of bad guys in our legacy, mentality, in every cell of our body and brain?

It is so hard to work with spades and hammer if you born to be a son of kings!

Unquestionably, we are all belonged to ancient Kyrgyz nation and identity, fixed in our common historical roots and sources, prevalent nomadic mentality, traditions and so on. There are so many things that united us: our beautiful nature and mountains, our unique positioning - right in the center of Eurasian supercontinent - in the green oathis surrounding by the great deserts where taken place the key pit-stops of caravans moved to and fro along the Silk Road which from the ancient times lingering West with the East. Our nomadic past, national folklore, the heroic epos "Manas" – all these things have formed and defined us as one nation, called Kyrgyz.

Every region of Kyrgyz Republic are very proud with the some or other historical events, remarks, parables or just of mentioning's and allusions bringing from epos "Manas" with the trepidation pointing such coincidences.

For example our Kara-Kulja district well known from our great epic narration as the favorite place and mountain resort where Manas with his 40 jigits-choros so loved hunting and resting. According with the epos, Kara-Kulja had exceptionally rich fauna, its mountains and slopes teamed with the specific kind of mountain deer's, called and featured as "black deer" – kara kulja – meaning as excellent deer's, compare with ordinarily species bigger, stronger and more attractive for hunting.

Really, the pastures and jailoo[17] of Kara-Kulja still keep their excellent conditions and qualities for bearing wildlife and livestock, even though our region also suffered from serious decrease of our nature and resources. The sheep, gouts, horses breading in Kara-Kuldja pastures well known for their best qualities and inhabitants of this region very proud with them. Of course, the meals and dishes prepared from such animals also have specific kara-kuljian qualities.

By the way I must say that our Kara-Kulja district very proud with the fact that epos "Manas" mentioned about such product as Ozgon red rice, which in reality originated from Kara-Kulja rice, grown up only on fertile lowlands at the edge of Kara-Daria which translated as black (rich) river.

Of course, every Kyrgyz preferred at the first rate such traditional our cuisines as kazy-karta, beshbarmak, byju, chychyck[18] – the delicious sausages, prepared from horses meal. However, we never forget about our, additional foods and dishes historically well-known and mentioned in various resources as Kyrgyz national dishes, like Kyrgyz plow, prepared from Kara-Daria rice and meat of local sheep. This famous eating long ago put in our mentality as one of the brandish

---

[17] Jailoo – the summer pastures, originated from word jai, mean summer.

[18] The popular Kyrgys meals and cuisines prepared from sheep's and horses meats.

dishes of South region of Kyrgyzstan and Kara-Kulja district. It's well known from old years that for the respected guests in Kara-Kulja will make the specifically delicious kind of plove - prepared from meat of deer, keklik, ular[19].

We are all belonged to one nation and culture, our root grown from one soil and one place, but we are rich with our differences and regional diversities.

These differences might be and must be used for our advantages, for uniting and enriching our culture, not to separate us from each other. Our lieders and governors must show clear respect to that features for the matter of support our unity and differences.

Sharip aba very respected Absamat Masaliev as the prominent Kyrgyz politic and honest man, who ruled by our country 5 years since 1985 to 1990.

"We cannot despise the fact that Kyrgyz nation divided for North and South regions - geographically, mentally and even historically, because in the last century the North part of Kyrgyzstan had a better opportunities for development on behave of next reasons, like: more stronger influence of Russian and Kazach cultures on North region, the problems with the transport communication with the capital of Kyrgyz Republic for the inhabitants of South region, which separated by great mountains and transregional automoibil road would built only in 1970 years, and modernized and covered with asphalt only in the years of our Independence.

No wonder that Northern Kyrgyzes looking slightly differently compare with southerners.

---

[19] Ular – the wild mountain turkey, exceptionally delicious for preparing the king's dishes; keklik - mountain partridge, very well for preparing excellent meal for respected persons and heads of company where you have worked.

Absamat Masaliev well understood these problems and his governing was very fruitful in term of making close our different regions and uniting them. He has never suffered from sectarianism and tribalism, he had never asked and interested from the people selected for the state duty and working - where they come from and what the tribe or region they represented?

He appreciated candidates according with their personal qualities as diligence, workability, honesty, grade level and for the gained experience. It might said that regional factor and sectarianism have not play any role in his time, because as lieder he despised such criterias for the making choice at all.

It was a decent and cohesive leadership, which was as good and compatible for such country as Kyrgyzstan, healthy for its wholeness and regional development. He equally looked for all regions and their problems and know how better solved them and how pulled and involved the local lieders and young generation for the various promising businesses and activities. That is why the years when he ruled by our country, were the years of fast growing a new generation of Kyrgyz elite – as at regional so at republican level also, almost wholly free from sectarianism and tribalism.

If the leadership of Absamat Masaliev will proceeding twice or even more longer than his 5 years of real governing, which had to be break off by dirty plot and intrigues, and he left in top of Kyrgyz states management, maybe the problem of Kyrgyz regionalism solved eventually and lost it's actuality at all for the future politician.

So it was the tragic mistake what happened in 1990 years when Absamat Masaliev was toppled from his position as the head of state and replaced by the Askar Akaev who not only 15 years left in power and ruined our economy, its firmament but also revived our old pains and heavily mental problems, pretending not to see the growing cancer of regionalism and sectarianism into body of Kyrgyz politic, culture, economy within the long years of his governance. Sharip aba was saying to have called the unlawful and shameful resigning of Absamat Masaliev as the biggest blunder of Kyrgyz political establishment in the first year of our independence.

Our country wants a president unapologetic about using power and way he can. But Masaliev had lack of experience of survive in tribal North and Bishkek, its capital and capital of state. His background of democratic leader and honest negotiator made him a deer in Jogorku Kenesh's headlights. It needs to say all these events happened in the exceptionally important second part of 1990 year, when defines the matter of highest order – who will be the first president of independent Kyrgyzstan?

Nevertheless, in any cause according with Sharip aba, every Kyrgyz, especially if he prepared himself for the governing service must be fight against regionalism and tribalism and conquered these evils in his soul. And the best way for reaching this aim – have to keep good attitude and relation between North and South of Kyrgyzstan personally, bring own impact for solving this question.

Sharip aba himself had to working all life to keep good friendly lings with the friends, colleges and relates from North region, not only with the some influential person and official bodies like Koshoev but with the ordinarily people also, with the retired officials, writers, artists, journalists and so on.

Of course we must love and respect our close environment, our family, and children but for the same reason we must also create the good relation with the far our friends, colleges, relatives.

His sons and daughters are also inherited the such traditions and got to strengthening various ties between North and South of Kyrgyzstan through maintaining friendship, cultural, educational lings and communications and political activity also.

As we well known the such sons of Sharip aba as Asylbek Jeenbekov and Sooronby Jeenbekov are played important roles in the party of SDPK, established by the president of Kyrgyz Republic Almazbek Atambaev, who said that in face of Sooronby and Asylbek he found out the truly and honest friends.

However, unless the leadership of Kyrgyz Republic willing to commit substantial reforms, it is impossible hope for the best future.

President also is the father of big family, that including seven large oblasts as his own sons and two beautiful major cities–daughters – Bishkek and Osh. The prosperity and future of this family depending wholly from his love, knowledge, decency, honesty, wiseness. If he able to do a good work, entire country will be happy, if not - his people will suffered, disgraced, and humiliated.

President was married to own country, and must be deeply respect and adore her. It's mean he married and fall in love to Democracy if he has really wanted provide the best governing, which unavoidable lead country and its people to peaceful and happy future and prosperity - from generation to generation.

The lesson for our time

We have little chances to win and change this fatal and wrong course for our independence, which too long passively and shameful held up by the predominant part of post-soviet governments and presidents. Without joining to one front of all democratic and pro-democratic forces of our country and creating the broad coalition of pro-west's movement we failed again and again into various catastrophes and calamities as a direct result of bad post-soviet habits and strong defining influence of authoritarian Russia and it total dominance in our outward and inward environment. Without strong belief to West and Democracy in hearts and souls and their guide and even patronage we have a little chances for better future.

So we need to join Kyrgyz nation through principles of democracy - women and men, representatives of south and north part of country, various tribes, the supporters of Usubaliev, Masaliev, Akaev, Bakiev, Atambaev.

Then we must involve in our union the Kyrgyzes who filling themselves close relate with the kalmaks, kypchaks, uygurs and so on.

Then created good attitude with the democratic lieders of next Diasporas

Russian, Ukrainian, Uzbek, Uygur, Dungan, Kazak, Korean, Jude, Turks and others.

Than broader forces and movements, we united, than better our future and hope for Democracy. However, it is not the easy task, which has demanded lot of love, tolerance and managing skills.

V

The lessons from Samara apa

What can we leave to our future what have to be as valuable and precious as our love, honesty and wisdom? What can be more consistent and dearer for really deep and passionate senses, which able to grant the generations with the increasing, developing and unfolding treasure of freedom and happiness than Democracy?

The mother-in-law of Democracy

Russia makes a deal with the every post-soviet state as jealous mother with her son, when he has created own family marrying to the beautiful lady of freedom, independence and democracy.

The old woman with the strong authoritative mentality in the very next day after bountiful festival and congratulations, started own big game and fight for her son, trying to rise him against young wife, searching ways for diminishing her power and attractiveness.

She burdened kelin with the various house works and lay down on her excessive demands, sometimes treating and pressing her mentally and psychically, hoping that her daughter-in-love after first years of marriage, honey moons, pregnancy and so on will eventually bump up against a hard ceiling of support of his husband, and that helped to slip him back to old rigid traditions beyond them kelin20 not be able to grow, gradually forgetting about democracy, social justice, human development and protections and others west's values, and eventually mother victoriously returned her previous influence and authoritarian power above dear son and through him against both of them.

That is why our people so loved this proverb: "Russia is our old mom, that so earnestly backed and kept traditions".

We urgently need to ditch or seriously reform some of our outdated traditions and try for more respect the principles of Democracy and universal human values.

The problem of gender inequality in Kyrgyzstan and many other Asian countries it is at substantial level the unsolved problems between two

---

[20] Kelin – fiancée, originated from Kyrgyz-Etruscan-old English gelin, means "the girl who coming to new home."

generation of woman - young woman, kelin, who entered after marriage into a family where mother-in-law took place leading position.

It is problem, which able to better solved only through nurturing and establishing the Democracy, which is an expression of pure love, honesty and decency.

-Samara apa, what was your mine secret that yours kelins so nice and kind - all of them? Why that is so? It is look as if you personally selected and found out every one of them?

Samara apa, gently smiling to my questions, told me:

-Not at all. My sons themselves did that kind of jobs, found out their preferences, fall in love and come to us together and we blessed them, made wedding ceremonies and so on. No one of these unions will not been dictated or even recommended by us or somebody else from relatives. They were themselves made a choice and did it well, all my daughters-in-love pretty good and lovely creatures, they are all close to me as my own daughters, God bless all of them.

Yes, really, in that reveal of Samara apa we find not even the small degree of embellishment so usually for our tradition. Many others mothers-in-love in our country could not create a good and harmony attitude with the daughters-in-love or do that job with the great efforts, fights and sacrifices. Often old woman liked one kelin and disliked others, cannot keep good balance or after happy marriage her son, she may become envious and fell in depression, and even ready make a threat for kelin and so on.

Why is that so? When one mother and woman well managed this process of creating new family and other didn't? Sometimes parent actively selected ultimate pair for their children helped them to make a good choice but nevertheless after wedding ceremonies and all fests and congratulations, cannot survived and live under one roof with the daughter-in-love?

Of course, there were a lot of problems and undiscovered things, which need for deep learning and investigation for make a final recommendation and good advises. Life is a very complicated thing. Sometimes a good man encountered with the worthiest woman and must to live together and vice-verse often a nice woman coupled with the rouge one for the entire life. We don't understand at full measure why such oddly and ugly thing happened in our reality but we have also well informed about modern law of Attraction and ancient Kyrgyz proverb - a good man inclined to be with the good ones and a bad man has sought the bad ones and things and found them.

Moreover, according with that law and point of view the two sides make create good mutual relation and understanding and peace in family if they will be equal to each other with the wiseness, tolerance and sagacity. If one side – kelin or mother-in-love - going to be feeling herself more knowable, informed and wise and lost a tolerance to other side - that is leading to misunderstanding, growing tension in family which might ended very badly, turn out to unstoppable battles, conflicts and even end up with a catastrophe. Mother starting suppress kelin or kelin in own turn announced war - and poor man and husband in such trouble situation often had feeling himself as between hammer and anvil.

Of course egoism, pure conceit and ambitions when every side firmly believed that "the truth on my side", "i was right, you made a wrong", "you must do what I said and all be OK" – such post-communistic mental notions, set of rules and recommendations have to inevitable going to the conflicts.

Samara apa and Sharip aba could create in attitude with the daughters-in-love so happy and warm environment based on great mutual respect, tolerance and kindness which so rarely have to observed in our life. Of course, this case might been a good lesson and example for learning and imitation by many other families - especially for young families and also as the matter for serious scientific research and disputation. Yes, for scientifically investigation and analyzing.

Does it exist in our world more serious question which so needs for fundamentally solution and scientifically investigation as the peculiar attitudes between kelin and mother-in-love and art of getting good and excellent understanding, harmony and love into family life? I think there is nothing compare them that is why I had not tire to sing hosanna for every wise old and young women have lived in peace and for Democracy.

About democracy

The essence of democracy is revealed in respect for every human being, in strong intention to create the decent conditions for full development of every one and society, regardless of their place of residence, age, race, gender, physical abilities, talent, or lack thereof.

All other ideologies, concepts and religion anyway only serve the interests of certain privileged groups, teaching and preparing them and their life and mission for the active or passive infringement of rights of others or majority in favor of selected minority and nurturing the base and root for the fundamental inequality and injustice.

The most astonishing thing is that all daughters-in-love of mother Samara are resemble to each other with their kindness, politeness and patience and deep respect to family values, not depending from origin and where lived their relatives – in North of Kyrgyzstan or in South, belonged to provincials or citizens.

The same we might say about sons-in-law whom also Samara apa loved as own children.

From the first day when her some or other daughter have married and come to home with husband, she gladly welcomed him, filling herself happy as if she has blessed by another child and son.

When Samara apa has guested at home of her daughter Gulaiym in Bishkek, she so enjoying by the heartily communications with her son-in–love Janysh that the talking usually lasted all night, until to dawn.

"Mother never told with me so long as with my husband,"- remembered Gulaiym.

By the way among the kelins of Samara apa we have seen Hyrila, the wife of Jusupbek, whose parents originated from north of Kyrgyzstan, living in town Sokuluk, placed in the west side of Chui valley on 30 kilometers from Bishkek along the state's main magisterial road, which lingered North and South regions together.

Among southerners still have existed some prejudices against kelins and wives that come from north region, the same things we might say about reflection of our citizens from North when we said about southern traditions.

Usually in south has widely distributed common opinion that kelin and wife from north had a strong character and bad temper, that they liked to do what they want to do and disrespected the many good Kyrgyz traditions.

However, in the case of Nurila, bar surprises, the matter is turn to be a quite different. As said the first kelin of Samara apa Mairam, "it's look as if she (Nurila) was specially shaped for our family, so kind, diligent and cohesive to Kyrgyz and our tradition she is."

But Samara apa all these happy coincidences explained with the next very simple and wise notation: "I am just love all my kelins, and maybe from that reason, they are all also answered to me with love and respect, have got me as their own mother.

Nobody has stopped the greatest force of nature

Authoritarian regime has deeply contradicted to the fundamental law of the universe - the law of love and attraction. Because such system involved citizens for the unnatural love to the leader of the nation and to the course he happen to supported.

Such love would be justified partly if the leader was a progressive person who pulled the country and its people into the bright future. But in more common case when the president is just the bad man who busy with the strengthening own power and nurturing hostility to the free world and dreams about returning to the Soviet Union, he is transformed himself and country to the absolute renegade of history, acting against fundamental principles of the world.

Nevertheless, no one also could cancel and despise the law of attraction and love. That is why we are all unavoidable moved toward West Europe attracted by the greatest forces. We know all that our world and universe have deeply predisposed for creating a good environment and worked according with the law of love and attraction with the great exactitude. And the love to the national leader and to all sort of dictatorship, including the Soviet Union — it's utterly unnatural phenomena, it's a wraith and intoxication of the past centuries, the results of tragic mistakes and incompetence and lack of knowledge will blew away out of window with the first breath of freedom.

Nurila said: "We are met with Jusupbek in Kiev where we graduated at state university. Since that time I knew the parents of Jusupbek, he introduced me to them when they visited to his son lived in Kiev. Knowing that I originated from north, they were not against our planning unity with Jusupbek. I had not heard and felt from my future mother and father any slightest degree of disagree or displeasure or some discomfort from our choice and decision. Late when I invited Jusupbek to Sokuluk before our marriage and introduced him to my parents, they were also not shown any disagreement and welcomed and blessed our unity but, nevertheless, my mother and father told me personally that I must be prepare for some problem in future. Yes, sure, we both with Jusupbek went through several serious tests. Who does despise that we have some problems due the regional dividing Kyrgyzstan for north and south and existing differences between traditions, cultural, educational levels and way of life of these parts?

Certainly I knew beforehand that since I marry to the south jigit[21] I must know well and keep the southern traditions, respect them and Jusupbek and his parents. My father–in-law and mother-in-law many helped me, assisted and supported until I adapted to the new for me environment. And it was not hard for me as for many other kelins who put in the similar circumstances. I want say especially about delicate attitude to that matter of my father-in-love, because from the first day this man very kind and polite received me in his family. It was clearly feeling even in his speech when he turned to me, he preferred use to the words and expressions common for north dialect. He had also expressed sincerely respect and honor to my parents and other close relatives.

---

[21] Jigit – the common name of young man (in positive meaning)

Honestly say Sharip-aba looked for me and my relatives differently, compare with other kelins. When my parents visited in south of our country, say, coming to Osh or Jalal-Abad, my father-in-love invited them to Kara-Kulja, without any way for failing or postponing this visit, at the honor of dear guests made a fest, toi in there. Of course, how such warmly attitude and lovely respect would not welcomed by me and touched my heart? So I am feeling myself happily living in such family and my parents also were happy seeing the happiness of their daughter. By the way from the warm attitude of my father-in-love to me, I am also going to change my nature, having to be more warm and kind to my sister and brothers and other relatives.

Admittedly these both persons - as my father-in-love so my mother-in-love also – have owed the some core parts of pedagogical faculties, inherited by the best of Kyrgyz traditions, when we told about good and wise principles on the base of family life. They have a waste knowledge, which helped them created and cemented such large, mutually well balanced, inwardly and outwardly harmoniously and friendly constituted family.

When I for the first time opened this kind of special and delicate warmness and kindness in attitudes between various members of that family, I thought it all created artfully, put on just for show, as that often taken place in some small societies, but late I were growing in my better understanding of features this family and could appreciated the wisdom, sagacity and diligence of its founders.

Of course such families and persons, who have had the similar properties are belonged to extremely rare, almost exceptional causes in our ordinarily life. The most of other families known nothing about and have not shared even small parts of its achievements.

Nevertheless, for my opinion, the main secret of such extraordinarily pedagogical skill of Sharip aba might be encapsulated by the next simple sentence – he gained great success due to his great honesty, justice and love, and everyone who will trying to do the same things in his family life, have reached in short and long-term the similar results.

When he visited to his kelins, his daughters-in-laws, he brought presents to every one of them, no one of them forlorn or disrespected with the quality or tests of some or other presents. Even in late years when he was retired and could not more make happy us with the expansive things, this man when meeting to us proceeded to bring some chocolates, candies and others similar items and equally distributed among us, not forgotten anybody, that so amazed us.

My husband Jusupbek has inherited many good sides of his father and mother. I can witnessed this notion with the next very simple comparison and even confirmation if you like more. In what rate I transformed to be a some kind of southern girls, at the same level my husband Jusupbek turned to be a northern jigit. That is marvelous metamorphose!

From this remark of Nurila the wise man or scientist might to open the door for the several valuable conclusion, even more some decent, foreseen and all reckoning politic will able to find long-termed solution optimal formula for making peace and stability in our country which have divided and torn now from such many hard problems.

-Honestly say, we have deal with the unique family and its founders, - told Janysh ake, the husband of Gulaym. – I were born and grew in modest provincial family and for make career and reach success in this life it was need many worked for. Except me all my other brothers and sisters are living in the same district and village where lived their fathers and forefathers and traditionally herding is their main business. Only I am alone move up, graduated, gained urgent experience and found place and work in Bishkek. Life was not cared and spoiled me in luxury but I were happy that God gave me so wise and foreseen and kind new parents like Sharip aba and Samara-apa. I just say them thousands thanks for their existence and for presenting me my dear wife Gulaym, for theirs sisters and brothers. With all the children of Sharip aba I am keeping good attitude but especially close to me the oldest son of aksakal Kantoro and the next Iskender who lived in our home when he studied in Bishkek university. He was a marvelous boy and we lost him so regretfully and tragically.

From the very beginning of that family couple, when Sharip and Samara married - in the hard post-war years at the middle of last century, - Samara apa respected as own child the little brother of Sharip, Abdylda, the son of Toktokan.

Abdylda was grown to a respect older now, as a head of big family, he is father of six children, and all of them are boys.

"In the days of my childhood, - he remembered,- our folk had quite the different mentality and tradition. Despite the hardship and common poverty, lack of knowledge and material resources, our people in past time were richer and healthier in soul and kept carefully the human relations and good attitudes.

For example, all people in our village lived as one big family; you were warmly welcomed in every home. Not so we have seen today, today we are all lived much more separately, despite the fact that our life is getting richer with more comforts and more safety, with the much more higher level of general literacy, when everyone might to read and write and lot of youngsters have a good, even excellent education and preparedness when some toddlers make create a wonderful things in PC - that is all OK. But, nevertheless, our people in the recent decades very fast going to lose any kind of interest for the mutual communication, respect and support each other and for the keeping a good relation even between close brothers and sisters".

It might to say that Sharip aba and Samara apa at their family life and attitude with other relatives have kept and saved these principles of mutual support, respect and warmness, which had formed and crystallized during the severely wars and pre-wars years. As in old good days, they lived closely and warmly with all brothers and sisters and their children —as one big family. As said Kyrgyz proverb, food that we eat and water, which we drink - from one source.

Look for example for this sheepfold, which built close to the house of Sharip, that contains fifty sheep. Generally my son Mars looks for the animals, provided them with food, water, cleaned building and so on. He studies externally in a commercial institute in Jalal-Abad. We were used to make all businesses together. That's why the achievements of every one of us turned to be as our general success and advance. I were personally with the help of my brother Sharip had graduated in Institution for the veterinary facility. And my son also has studied thanks for old son of Kantoro, who is the rector of Jalal-Abad commercial institution and have been for me as my close brother.

Together with Kantoro, Jusupbek and all others brothers and sisters and their children we were joined our land properties. As a result we were have own the 12 hectares of land, and I am and my children appointed as the farmers and owners. On this base, we will planning to create a good farm and I know that it is a good idea and promising undertaking. Because I am constantly feeling the support from my relatives. I am himself the man blessed for such kind of work and have a six children and all of them boys and loved the farm works and in warm friendly terms between each other's which so valuable in such sort of works as farming. When comes time for the work with soil, tilling, Sooronby provided the technic assistance with the tractors, oils, fertilizations and so on. Sharip aba himself also involved to this business and make a guidance and help us when it needed.

Honestly said we well trained and educated for common life in prosperity and welfare. Whenever need to me to bring sheep, I will bring it from this sheepfold and every one of us done the same things. Of course, such collective life have a lot of problems and duties but into that great family, all their members equally loved hard work, very diligent and honest. Sharip ake himself despite the retiring and old age actively involved to this business and united us and show to us how need to work for the common interest and prosperity.

Needless to say that Samara apa and Sharip aba from the first days as one by one married their children bringing at home kelins, have spent lot of energy, love and warmness for creating good relation with then, make their new lives as more comfortable and well protected as possible based on mutual respect, understanding and love.

When youngest son married and come to home with Baktygul and going to be forming the new relations and refreshing and correlating all previous schemes of behaving within large family, Samara apa asked his daughter Gulaym assisting her on her deal with newcomer. "If I suddenly lost temper and said something what make hurt Baktygul even in smallest measure, please, interfere to matter on the side of new kelin."

Father Sharip also liked watching how Samara apa make a deal with her kelins, and when he has seen how Samara sitting on the blanket surrounding by kelins and communicated with them, liked to joke upon his spouse - look for her mother-in-love, she so enjoyed in the company of her kelins.

It is a words of wise man, who was the father of 11 boys and girls. He not only spent lot of time and energy for their growing, educating and preparing for active life but proceeding this kind of job and support when they starting own life, engaged in marriages. He assisted them and created a life-long good relation with the all children–in-law and their parents and relatives.

Many father could not to create good relation with the one or two family counterparts, even could not survive and find compromise with own wives; think about so many problem around us and then show respect to the people who able to do such sort of works.

"We married with Kantoro (the oldest son of Sharip aba) at 1969, - remembered Mairam, the great daughter-in-love of Samara apa. – In 1970 after finishing to study in Kyrgyz state university in Bishkek, I returned to the home of Sharip aba in Ozgon. Two years we lived together with the parents of my husband. It was a difficult time for the family, because all children, except Kantoro, were young. Of course, Sharip aba worked hard in prestigious job and provided the big family with all needs and spends and well done that. However, so many children have not left any time for rest for both parents. It is now all looks wonderful, when these boys and girls grew, educated and lived with own small families and succeed in various branches and entertainings. But in that days, when I at first arrived to the home it was a quite different story. The big house did not know a peace at all, even for minute, full of noise and din.

I missing my mother-in-love and decided to stay at home and share her house works and duties. Let I have not chance to make own professional fortune and work after graduating in university as a teacher. Now, after so many years when I have seen our big family and good affairs and mutual respect so deeply planted and rooted there, I did not regret about lost opportunities. I was deeply integrated to this family, learned and owed so many worthy things from Samara and Sharip, that it all add up enough to feel me fine and happy in such environment. Now I pretty understood a lot of things and wished for my children and grandchildren let they also grown and lived in such level of family tolerance, mutual support and warmness and had keep the same happiness, comfort, harmony, protection, and safety into own family lives.

Sharip and Samara with daughters.

In the hot July of 1970 after finishing the graduate at the Kyrgyz state university in Bishkek, when I received blue diploma about my high education, after two week I was born my first baby – Gulnas. My father- in-love was very happy, he arrived to Bishkek and come in time at maternity hospital when I was ready with firstborn go out. He gave baby to his hands and we together went out to airport and from there flying to Osh and from there on taxy moved to Ozgon. Until we got to Ozgon he was so happy holding the baby in his hands, not bringing him to me nor to my husband.

Why our universe, sun, planet, physical laws are so precisely tuned and created so marvelously for our life and perception? Because, the modern scientists Brian Green answered, they primarily yield conditions which was so suitable for our kind of origin and our evolution, which lead to reality that so familiar and dear for us.

Why the big family of this man was growing in such fruitful environment and reached so many advantages?

Because, parents created the family on the firmament of justice, love and self-realization and yield the same principles, laws and conditions which needed for such spectacular appearance.

Sharip aba lived and worked in terms of deep love and democracy, used these things with practical way, had been lovable father and wise democrat - in real action and attitude, he was been epitome of such excellent principles in his family, working environment, in communication with the relatives, friends and colleges.

The miracles of truly love

Remember, when we loved sincerely somebody
more than ourselves,
we were all going to be looking for as truly Democrat,
marvelously transformed and refreshed
and inspired by the great power of love.
We not only stopped to plan and act wrongly,
we even expelled out such things from mind and soul wholly
and really able to do something extraordinarily,
something heroically
ready for sacrifice ourselves
for the benefits of dear one.

Thus the magic of love, Democracy and truly greatness
go on above egoism and autocracy,
when person forget totally about own priorities.

So when every human society
and every member of it
learned to love and respect each other and all of them
with the same degree and responsibility
which well known for those who loved,
the democracy institutions
starting make up a wonderful miracles
in our reality
unraveling all their hidden Quantum potencies and powers.

The space, time and metric of our deep desires and wishes

I am coming to next conclusion and expressed it when many people asked me, why did your children grow in so warm, friendly and cohesive terms in attitude to each other and respect their parents? I thought all explained, maybe, by the strong will of my kayin-ene, the grand mother-in-law. She had not child and all her life desperately suffered from loneliness. She dreamed about having many children, to be pregnant and bring new lives into the world but God for some unexplainable reason didn't give the poor woman what she asked and desired most of all.

But the woman growing older and older also never giving up in her ultimate desire, she proceeded asking children until her last years and days come, whispering at sunset the next praying - O my God, you are not blessed me by children, not gave me the chance to enjoy with the first move of tinny fetus in my body that gradually growing to get to be born, not filled my home with the offspring's and I have not to keep hate to you for all these hopeless and fruitless long years of my asking and waiting. Yes, I know that I am soon dying and return to you and not left child behind. But let give to other my relatives and to their children what you not given to me. Bless them with the multiple young generation and let them to be happy and grateful to you for your gifts.

Father–in-love was also lonely person and very devoted to the idea about children. Even when he grazed livestock on nearest hills he dreaming about many grandsons and granddaughters. I thought their strong intentions, prays and requests turning up to God have eventually reached and realized through us.

At this point, we may come to very interesting and promising conclusion after such marvelous excursion to past life of Samara apa and its revelation. As said the famous Kyrgyz proverb "jakshy tilek – jarym yrys", means literally - "a good wish is a half of happiness". Admittedly, it is a great truth, which had sent to us from our wise ancestors. We are all wanting and asking the good wishes for ourselves, as just as precious as plenty of money, excellent health and many others happy returns, that is quite naturally things and good human habits. However it is principally valuable when you have got to shape your wishes - done that with the right way, harmoniously arranged them for others too - not only for yours person and even yours family and in broadly scale for yours society and country but for the world at all.

If such well-balanced and consistent desire, wish or aim have very strongly possessed by some or other person or even better by group of persons, transformed and indoctrinated in their mind to the life-long supremacy, of course, such dreams are going to materialize with some or other way. It is only matter of time to get to transcendence for such sort of wishes, which quite desirable and extremely important not only for separate human who wished it, but for other part of relatives and environment.

That is why your wishes and life-long aims if they will not contradicted with the wishes and aims of yours others relatives - close and far, if they must been ever in harmony with all of them and world, they have a good chance for realization.

However, the life of Sharip aba and Samara apa and their lineages, as the story of their family benefits and achievements have revealed another background of that ancient truth.

If you in yours will and desire have to expressed deep and ultimately respect and honor not only for your present environment but for yours past and future environment and generation - as deep and far as possible – if your desires and wishes very well harmonized and settled in such eternal space and metric - God or Highest Intellect might to blessed you with the enormous surplus – 10 or even 100 folds more than you asked for.

So I am too learned from Samara apa and Sharip aba and their wise forefathers and foremothers and present generation and future offspring's now going to ask for our next generation, for our coming children and grandchildren the stability and peace and competent and honest government.

Let Kyrgyzstan will create a decent and strong democratic society, which able to provide the long-standing stability and strong protection from various calamities, wars, cruel adventures and other stupidities of ignorance in rule. Let our country constituted itself with so respect and powerful way and self-expression in world arena as Israel, Switzerland and other prospered nations. Let our state close integrated with the honest and decent states and avoid of all fatally bad and dangerous outdated regimes, strongly protected itself from them, until they were too find way leading to a communities of prosperous and democratic nations.

Sharip and Samara, 1975.

VI

The geopolitical view

In style and substance Sharip aba showed himself to be a distinctive unreconstructed old-school party member. As many other our representatives of old soviet generation, who worked in states services and various leading positions, he respected Communists ideology and its system of governing. He never had been abscessed neither by political ideology, neither by religion but know how extracted and utilized with practical way the better parts of both of them. Communist party of USSR banned many religious rituals and traditions, announced them as the opium of people and tried create the entire atheistic society.

Of course, such states workers and servicemen as Sharip Jeenbekov could not criticize and oppose to some clearly excessive doctrines of totalitarian party, like demand not believe to God if you want to join to party of bolshevic but many our wise people as Sharip can make the best, keeping distance from any kind of extremities from both sides. He not stopped to believe to God but thanks for Marxists ideology clearly have seen the many negative aspects of traditional religion and Kyrgyz mentality. He proceed believe to God but did it in soul, hiding this fact. From the other hand he as communist believe to its ideas and understood the progressively influence of soviet system for the many aspects of Central Asian region.

-We are learned lot of things, - told Sharip aba, - thanks for soviet regime and USSR lieders and theirs long-termed economic and political activities. As told remarkable about that positive influence the great Kyrgyz poet Toktogul, who lived and wrote his poems before and after the October Revolution in his famous poem "Who we were and who we are now". Kyrgyzstan was locked Asian country, without any access to European culture, technological achievements, education and so on – these all things brought to us through Russia. But if in Tsarist Russia we had been doomed for stagnation, assimilation and extinction as heavily suppressed colony, after October Great revolution situation changed and Sharip Jeenbekov as many our other representatives of old generation, believed for that fundamental doctrine of Communist party that she brought new hopes and blessings to all workers, enslaved masses and suppressed nations had lived into Russian empire.

Yes, sure among short pauses between revolution, civil wars, collectivization, WWII and other calamitites Soviet regime trying to do the best for the workers and peasants who sincerely believed to socialist ideas and calls of Bolshevik lieders and massively propaganda. Particularly gullible were small nations like a Kyrgyz people, who had suffered heavily in the last years of Russian Empire from its cruel colonial politics in the end of WWI, going through mass massacre of 1916 years when Russian Kazaks killed nearly 150 000 of Kyrgyz's population on the north of Kyrgyzstan. Communist's lieders that come to power after 1917 proclaimed war against Russian tsarism and its supporters and could luckily positioned and camouflaged own neo-imperialism of Bolsheviks establishing a completely new government and utterly new ideology as the state of workers and peasants which created for protect them from exploitations. But in reality this new state was filled with the same awful and outdated content and grown on the ground of injustice, violence and turn out the country even further from Democracy, cutting out and trumped down the sprouts of open society that gradually accumulated in Russian society in second part of XIX century.

Nevertheless, into the short historical time the country did the big leap ahead through industrialization to the modern form of management in agriculture, creating heavy and light industry, building hydro energetic and successfully implemented a program of combat with the illiteracy of population, lived at Central Asia and all other regions of USSR. It was a very strange world, where great economical achievement and industrialization mixed with the great terror and horror.

Of course, when I spoke with Sharip aba, it was a first year since the USSR unexpectedly collapsed and Kyrgyzstan gained the real independence. In that time the authority of Communist party was seriously suffered in post-Soviet area and worldwide. But older generation and substantial part of entire population proceeding to keep respect to the USSR and Communist party and remembered this past time with the gratefulness.

When I asked him which country should be the best partner and friend for our young independence and economic revival after collapse of USSR deeply integrated lings, maybe, China, our greatest neighbor, my father recommended me to give him such suggestion, because Kara-Kulja district bordered with the China and through this valley going one of the ancient brunch of Silk Road and Kyrgyzes lived there plaid active role in trade between China and other countries of Central Asia, for my astonishment Sharip aba decidedly despised any deep relation with China. "This country and its people are quite different from our country and people, and honestly say we never expect nothing good from them".

And such reaction is still typical for our old and middle aged generation. "Only Russian Federation and Russian might be for our people and country the best friend and partner, we have had deep historical roots and our mentalities identical for many aspects".

Interestingly, that his son Asylbek, who then in the beginning of 90 years actively involved in business and trade with the cotton, tobacco, oil and had a good achievement (today he is established as one of influential member of Kyrgyz Parliament – Jogorky Kenesh) also deeply sheared the opinion of his father.

He said me in an interview which I got in that time, when I asked him - what need to do for our government at first place for reaching peace and stability in our region and country - "The deep and good relation with the Russia on the level of strategic partnership, maybe opened military Russian base in the south region of Kyrgyz Republic and then demand from Uzbekistan to keep our right for water resources and paying for them. All our close neighbors - Uzbekistan, China, Tajikistan, even deeply related Kazakhstan with some or other way and level make a threat for our independence. Only Russia looks as neutral state for us and superpower, who really able to help us, if we keep good attitude with."

Yes, it right. But for Kyrgyz Republic also exceptionally valuable task is the creating strategic partnership with the USA and all other West's countries, and maybe find out compromise between Russia and West in our Kyrgyz soil. The military bases of two superpowers, which presented in our country together not so far and make up the first step for friendly cooperating with each other – it was a best possibility for diminishing tension between two worlds and strong guarantee for our safety and independence. Alas, we were lost this unique historical chance in 2010 year after April revolution, when the new lieders of Kyrgyzstan, coming to power with the help of Putin, under pressure of Kremlin must go to expelling US airbase deployed in "Manas."

By the way, oldest son of Sharip aba Kantoro, the rector of University of business and commerce in Jalal-Abad looked differently for such sensitive political subject. His university has worked in deep cooperation with the universities as Russia so Turkey, West Europe and he personally as Doctor of economic science (PhD) deeply respected the great achievement of modern Western technologies and theoretical advances in economic area. In the wall of his cabinet of rector of University hanged the pictures of all laureates of Nobel Prize in economic branches and under every picture given the short inscription of their work and discoveries for which they were honored.

Of course according with modern view and conception of international safety, for surviving and creating better future for our independence and prosperity Kyrgyz Republic must be in close and friendly term with all global superpowers equally – with Russia, USA, China, European Union, Arabian states, Turkey, Iran, India, Israel.

Central Asia has looked long into Europe through Russia

I am sure without the massively support of West, Kyrgyzstan will never be established as an independent and prosperous state.

Many representatives of older generation have said about the same thing, but differently in relation to the Russian, that Kyrgyz have not become civilized nation without Russian, Soviet power.

But if we cast keen view to such historical affection and love of Kyrgyz and other small Asian nations toward Russia, its culture and mentality, we find out again that our people attracted by the same best part of Russia - its wests mentality, close historical and mental link with

Europe. Figuratively saying Asians have looked to the West through Russia, searched West through this great Universe.

All convinced westerners and old generation, that tend to be pro-Russian and those I am mentioned above, totally agree with one point – without Wests civilization and democracy, we will not survive. For many of our elders Russia and the Russian people associated primarily with the Europe, although the Russian authorities within last 300 years had butting with European civilization, seeking to build up own "unique Eurasian civilization."

The very fact that Kyrgyz and other small nations so baked onto Russia, this is a merit of small part of Russian people and its mentality that defined as pro-Western and pro-European, despite the heavy contra-propaganda and opposition.

Asian part of Russia, which today totally dominated and nurtured by Kremlin propaganda and, according with polls, supported by 80 percent of the population. But this part, instead of attraction, has strongly repulsed all other Asian nations inside Russia and surrounding it and in other parts of world. No one takes such "Russian civilization" and all fear and deny it and this is thoroughly natural and healthy reaction of the World who searching peace and stability.

The fundamental constant of love

My English and I am very well fitted
for Quantum world's laws and weirdness,
to live, communications and love here
in strange comfort, extra vividness and happiness,
so far from classical standards and rigidness.
In the world where you not find any fixed position, shape
and room for harsh 3 dimensions,

where the time not existed at all
goes forward and backward
and changed rapidly with the others measures for distances.
It is really amazing reality
tightly packed with the primarily wonders and possibilities
and great powers and speeds.
And where love so adorable, perfect and great
in its limitless unraveling in Superposition.
Yes I am, my English and my love
for Quantum world very well fitted,
where seems other constant not yielded and existed.

Lessons have taken from Superposition

The two greatest blunders, which made by our tribal lieders in latest 200 years of Kyrgyz history

1. First strategic mistake. In the middle of XIX century, when Senate of Kyrgyz tribal lieders due to the strong pressure of Russian empire to the northern tribes forced to agreement about joining Kyrgyzstan to the Russia. Majority despised another competitive option – creating union with the China. Kyrgyz lieders firmly believed that Russian empire have much more perspective as strategic partner for Kyrgyzstan, in as much as some of tribal chiefs were bribed, some attracted by great promises for leadership under the Russian protectorate.

But the head of Kyrgyz Senate – Alymbek datka, the most influential among Kyrgyz southern tribes and the truly lieder of all nation, suggested to all Kyrgyz tribal lieders the 3th geopolitical option, which looks more risky and promising also. Alymbek datka lobbied the 40 Kyrgyz tribal lieders to join and make one coercive choice to get under the Engelchins (English) protectorate.

"If we find protection under the Engelchins Empire, which now leading war in Afghanistan and partly occupied this land, it will be much simple for us in future to return again our freedom and independence. However, if we joined to Orus padysha (Russian tsar), it will be too hard to get out of his strong embrace. Engelchins forces and government not so strongly attached to our region as Orus and in addition to, this far state and nation more advanced, efficient, civilized and updated and able to better learn our people and state throughout our joining and collaboration".

But lieders of Kyrgyz tribes on the north of Kyrgyz land had got such extraordinarily suggestion of the king of Kyrgyz nation with cold blood, just agree as subordinates. Because some of them despise it for political reason, wanting to deteriorate the power of Alymbek datka and even topple him, others decided in soul waiting for the common course upon this subjects, and among northern influential lords had been lieders who separately and secretly from others and Kyrgyz nation make a deal with the Russian emissaries in region, "managing protection" for his own tribe under Russian tsar and protectorate.

We do not know clearly, what happened later with the Alymbek datka. According with the general version of Kyrgyz soviet historiography, the situation in Kokand kaganate has critically worsened after the treacherously murder of Alymbek datka by own southern competitors, who also trying to be on position of Kyrgyz king and head of Kokand kingdom and creating own diplomatic and geopolitical games. But according with the other sources, finding in the archives of Uzbekistan, Alymbek datka killed in the battle with the Russian army, nearly Shimkent town.

And this project - maybe the most promising and historically well-grounded and wise - of joining Kyrgyz nation and entire Central Asia under the protectorate of British kingdom was closed.

2.The second great blunder was happening in 2010 years, after April revolution (or April overplot), when our new government decided expelled US-military airbase deployed in our land under the heavily pressure of Russian government. As a result, the Kyrgyz Republic instead of joining to the West and World forced to enter into Custom Union. Headed and forced again by Russia, trying to turn back the wheel of history and restore USSR.

Really it's very hard to get out from our enslaved past in the spot of great geopolitical game into Central Asia.

VII

If you want to getting rich

-I were often asked by certain kind of questions, - told me Sharip aba, - like "What is the secret of being happy and prosperous? What kind of job, program, strategy and tactic we must keeping for reaching these aims?"

There is only one answer for such questions – make a good service and job for your people, being strongly intended and motivated for such purposes and throughout that gaining respect and love of community. If you diligent and stubborn in long-term, trying to do the right things for your environment and lot of people, such things as happiness, success and wealth come and attached to you with own way.

Those who wanted to find prosperity, richness and money in abandon quantity have to learn less think about such things and more about good works and making the best service for people.

Lot of capable men around us has primarily and exclusively thought about money and personal welfare and less about work and if such person involved in business or job for state, he is going make money with the increasing number of ways, forgetting about responsibilities, laws and so on. Of course, such business soon stacked or leading to the other more unpleasant results, like bankruptcy, money laundering, bribing and others. Greediness, sordid aims and dishonesty are created many obstacles on the way of self-realization as for individual person so for community and group of certain people who planned to make something valuable but turned with wrong way and failed to reach the success.

Although Sharip aba never belonged to the business class and make a commercial deals, he had many qualities of successful managers, like diligence in everyday works and duties, strong intention for the studying and gaining useful and applicable knowledge combined with big heartiness, tolerance, wiseness, capability to predict, foreseen lucky events and avoid bad things. As a result Sharip aba and Samara apa have reached to so great level of self-realization and happiness as barely able other our luckiest businessman, philanthropists and politics reached for.

They have established so big and prosperous family association, which included the dozen families of children and grandchildren, predominant part of them found themselves and make own businesses and deals very luckily.

Admittedly, it was a great job! Look around carefully and trying to find out another such extraordinarily example and achievement taking place in modern history of Kyrgyz family! Where and when among Kyrgyz families you observed such harmony, love, mutual respect and mutual understanding and tolerance! In striking contrast with that family we have seen a great number of distracting families, not understanding each other and going far from each other close relatives, brothers and sisters! Generation gap between fathers and children also tend to be broader and broader. Parents have not time, energies, desire and, by the way, the certain kind of knowledge for creating close and warm communications with the own children. And the next generation from babyhood and offspring has growing in odd condition of lack of heartily welcome and parental warm attitude and love. Such cool and unhealthy environment conformed eventually the cold blooded, meticulous, scrupulous and frustrated members of family those know not neither the art of respect older nor the good jobs with own children, when his time to come. That all leading to many discomfort and tragic events in our life and community, weakening and derailing the very foundation of our society and state.

Such life-long job for establishing healthy, happy and prosperous family might be comparing in some extend with the creating immortal masterpiece, a great novel or some inspiring picture. Even more such art of parents looks greater, with more sense, values, responsibilities and returns for life. Because the great painter, even if we mentioned the truly genius, has left behind the excellent works, then the good parents left as own legacy the good children and good persons, who able to do a good job for people and life. Who know which one of that tasks and missions is more greater and bearing more responsibilities and returns for private and common system of values?

It is very interesting that Kyrgyz society as any other one in East and predominant part of the World has starkly committed to tradition, this other word for mediocrity, to indoctrinating it in our mentality as something wise and right thing and way of life which lead us not only to survive and safety but to greatness also. What a poor mind we have got as our lieders and teachers! The mediocrity is prevailed everywhere – in politics, religion, history, culture, in family life and most of all in national traditions. Everywhere the central point is that – keep the middle place, swim close to the middle of pack, not going ahead and not left behind.

Sharip Jeenbekov as ordinarily Kyrgyz man also was been devoted deeply to our traditions and kept them carefully, which look often almost unbearable for ordinarily people. But this man had had the additional capacity in its purity and extremely fresh quality - he loved his family and children from all his heart and this love deeply imprinted in his sole, life, mind and manifested the wonderful things in reality.

He had energy takes to be the best in that specific area and business. And all his children have to following his way, keeping his principles and multiplying father's achievement, respect and honor.

Sharip Jeenbekov with the grand-children.

VIII

Father's lessons

As said Kyrgyz proverb, until you have farther – learn more, make a trip as often as possible, wandering, accumulate your knowledge's and awareness about the world.

Sharip aba gave such possibilities for all his children, but once more, he trying inwardly and outwardly created the good environment and soil for his offspring's further, for their lifetime stretching prosperity and happiness when they left without parents and their guideline.

He helped them to be a good educated men, who learned in prestigious universities and the same time deeply respected our national traditions and many practiced on specific studying and performing what our people called as the art of being human – communication with various people and make friends from them. Sharip aba himself was a great master of such sciences and all his life created the good environment for his children. Even the fact that he kept good relation with the so many influential persons throughout country, - in south and north region and beyond its borders - said about the same strategy: he invited such influential persons like Koshoev to Kara-Kulja and make fest in their honor, because hoped for good lings between next generation – he hoped for strong leverage on them, their friends and relatives and others person in North to make the life of his children more comfortable and hopefully in future.

According with Bo Eason, people in life sentence involvement have power to do anything. They filled better themselves, had to not veiling and complaining as others prisoners, who have got here just for couple of years or little longer. They have to great success in memory training, chess playing; have reached astonishing skill in handmade arts and able to digging so deeply, diligently and with great mathematical preciseness through concrete wall, creating a neat long-stretched hole which one day will go outside into freedom. What is mean to be a lifetime sentenced to prison or committed to some work, mission!

And Sharip aba was committed for such lifetime activity as a good, diligent and respectful parent and made a such big progress that we are all see now. If he had been from the beginning a light-minded man, husband and father with the unbalanced soul and various uncontrolled desires, he of course, lost himself among vanities and triflers of the life.

So do I in my own way committed also in life-sentence into Superposition, have destined with the same diligence and stubbornness as this kind man that all his life cared about safety, prosperity and future of his children and family, I am too cared about the best of reality and wonderful outcome for my people and country, where Kyrgyzstan has strongly established itself among the great states and most influential nations, like US, Israel, Switzerland, Japan, Iceland and others like these happy states and nations.

We need such lieders as Abraham Lincoln, Alymbek datka, Ishak Razzakov, Isa Achunbaev, Bokbasar baatyr, Nookon baatyr, Asanbay baatyr who able for great projects and works. What we have now is Jogorku Kenesh and our deputies whose main talent seems to be pulling concerned faces as numerous serious events and challenges in a lifetime events occur.

Time to stop the petty politics and come up with a real worked strategy---big thinking is needed, a plan for the next 100 years or more.

Our past lieders and heroes achieved this on numerous projects---our current pygmies are obsessed with point and money scoring rather than problem solving.

Kumtor and other big investments and companies

If such gigantic risky investments as the gold mining works and production on Kumtor site in far corner of Ussyk-Kul valley were diverted to a massively growing small businesses and entertainments together with green culture and practices rush, the reward would be immense and Kyrgyzstan reputation as a vanguard not a laggard on modern economy and its advanced strategies and reforms are would be invaluable.

About big business and politic

The big business has not to come to power if we wanted totally excluded the so-called conflict of interests. Look what happened with our small enterprises just in one area, when our cabinet of ministers headed for several years the man who always forces own business. In the short time 20 Milles Company in our country closed, banned by government verdict, 17 of them in South of Kyrgyzstan. Hundreds of people lost their livelihoods and a large number of farmers who grow corn could not to process it into a cheap meal. Such mistakes on government level fueled a new wave of mass migration our citizens to the Russia and Kazakhstan and far beyond them.

That is direct consequences of our strategy of economic development, which was prepared and carried out by the our elite of rich and superrich men, that totally domineered in government and parliament, the same representatives of big companies and oligarchs, among them key role plays the supporters and cofounders of the Russian big states companies, like Gazprom.

On the verge of a full stop is the oil refinery in Jalal-Abad. In general, the whole idea of the construction of the new oil producing plant Joongo in Kara- Balta, in the north of Kyrgyzstan, where we have not a crude oil reserves and pressure on existed oil refinery in Jalal-Abad and Kyrgyzstan in Kochkor-Ata, where we have a lot of oil reserves, but prime-minister banned to refine it in place, suggesting carrion them into the North through mountainous road stretching for 500 kilometers - that is the bitter fruit of truly sectarian and irresponsible economic activities.

Let appreciate our truly brethren

Who are the truly relatives and brethren for us? Of course, the citizens of all democratic countries worldwide –Americans, Japans, Englishmen, Germans and so on - because they are represented of free states and born in freedom and certainly respected our freedom also, native language and independence. That is a quality of their nature and they have bringing to our land peace, prosperity and better future.

Who are the main enemies for us? Those who despised and hated our freedom and independence and our hope for democracy and better future, trying to bring us out of West's values and spend lot of energies and efforts for making enemy from them.

In Christianity and Islam, as in any other religion, those who believed, created own circle, trying to be between coreligionists as close as relatives, even named each other as brothers and sisters. Often religion has demanded among own people even more strong sense of closeness than closeness of belonging to one nation, citizenship and even family.

In terms of appreciating democracy, it is even much more valuable for every society, nation and person. Because democracy values are much more related and originated from truth than any other religious doctrine in the world.

That is why, we are also need at first-rate search, receive and dear the representatives of free worlds – from USA. UK, Japan, Switzerland and so on, make up deal and communication with them, stick to them, respect and love them, because they know the great truth and well-practiced on it.

Only after that we must to create attitude with the surrounding us non-free worlds, with our neighbors, relatives, citizens - again among them searching at first those who respected and loved democracy and West. It is very simple select such persons, communities and states - all of them show the truly respect and love to yours freedoms, independence, native language, because they were born and originated from eternal sources of freedom and democracy.

How old generations received October revolution and Communist party activities

What wonted to get communist lieders and what they really got?

The essentially declared aims and plans all without exceptions failed, degraded and distorted and the great country was going through cruelest decades of calamities, starvation, wars and repressions.

But why many Kyrgyz peoples and representatives of many others nations have still kept good remembrance about this harsh times and USSR? It is not only matter of nostalgia about young years, when our old generation survived, married and cares about children and their future in "the prison of nations."

The founders of USSR were been not bad politics and for Kyrgyz people and many others will prepared some sweeteners, they gained some profits and even relatively privileges which varied from one nation to other.

It is necessary to pay attention to the fact, that Kyrgyz nation especially severely suffered right up before October Revolution in 1916 years, when Russian Kazak's killed nearly third of Kyrgyz population. Communist come to the Central Asia as the savior of small nations from the colonial, genocidal politic of Tsarist Russia with the promises to bring freedoms, democracy, independence and liberty. Of course, that was all propaganda.

From the very beginning, Bolsheviks and their lieders only declared economical and political reforms - in reality quickly supplanted even worse and crueler dictatorship.

At the first days after October Revolution theoretically there existed smallest chance to go with the path of democracy, but it was a dead hope from the beginning. Revolution lieders didn't like much these principles, preferring only playing with them to make a full the broader mass and international societies. All real questions and problems Kremlin commissars decided with the powers and weapon and through uncompromised fight with the enemies of October.

As a tragic result of such collectively maddening the great country where lived hundred nations had emerged to the long running tumults, troubles and violence.

Admittedly, the Red lieders stopped reforms not starting them – and consequences were fatally for all nations, majorities and minorities who lived in USSR. Prison of nation remained in steadfast position even if top elite completely changed.

But why so many people proceeded to positively apprehend October Revolution and so attached with soul and heart to that historic event? Was the October revolution a really revolution, meaning deep change in the form of governing from the despotic regime toward freedom and democracy?

Since the beginning of these events, our world had many really great and successful revolutions, which lead countries in right direct. It was a post war transformation in Germany and Japan, Italy, South Korea, Singapore, successful transformation Spain from dictatorship to democracy.

Many good examples of successful transformation gave us the modern history after collapse USSR. I mean the best transformational practices of such nations of post-soviet bloc like Estonia, Poland, Czech Republic and many other countries.

Kyrgyzstan has had a rich history of such heroic attempts to create new society of freedom and democracy. In short time of our independence we have had two such events: March revolution of 2005 and April revolution of 2010.

But, alas, in both cases our people and society failed in attempts of launching the deep democratic transformation as did it many country before us in Europe and Asia.

But such practice of tragic failures of course not forgiven for our politics but may helped us better understand, why failed the Great October revolution hundred years before us.

Of course, if October Great revolution would have created the truly democratic USSR, it would be the great blessings for all nations and people inhabited this waste region of world.

Instead of free society and democracy, after October revolution very fast established one of the most severely and cruel dictatorship that humankind ever known. And our world sunk for 70 years for geopolitical confrontation, suffering and balanced on the verge of total destruction mainly because the October Revolution produced the large copy of North Korea called Stalinist USSR with the claim for the world hegemony and Red terror.

Thank for own failed revolution Kyrgyz people have had a magic glass which helped to better understand what happened 100 years ago in Russian, in first days and years after revolution, cast the look for these events through what happened in Kyrgyzstan 5 years ago.

April revolution in Kyrgyzstan had been even more heroic and bloody than Great October revolution if we compare assault of Zimni Palace on Senate plats of Petrograd at 1917 years with the horrific clashes between people gathered to coming out and government forces in Ala-Too square at 7 April 2010 years in Bishkek. Kyrgyz revolution in the first and decisive phase of seizing power substantially outnumbered October revolution with the number of sacrifices in the day of revolution 15 people killed in Senates plats and nearly 90 in Ala-Too square hundred years later.

But who needs the numbers, we turn opinion for the real changes after two revolutions

Alas, despite the mountain of promises, pathetic speeches and pamphlets as Great Russian Revolution so great April Revolution too both failed.

In both cases, the democratic parliamentary system of governing with the separations of powers, independent judges, media, and honestly functioning election had not being established. As Lenin and Stalin dodged and fooled the society promising it the best future and perfectly working government the same thing has happened twice with Kyrgyz people after March revolution of 2005 and April revolution of 2010 years.

At first we have seen as revolution lieder Kurmanbek Bakiev quickly transformed from democrat to authoritarian president and then as another democrat Almazbek Atambaev could not create really working parliamentary democracy.

And even before them, when rise to power our first independent president Askar Akaev in 1990 he also came to power with the promise to create democracy and we had seen as his regime gradually went to down instead of democracy toward strengthening more personal power and influence.

Yes our history abandoned with the failures of our presidents and their good guys and inner circle and advisers but such rich practice might to help us better understand not only our history, its drams and tragedies and crashed hopes but also the global events in our hemisphere in span of last centuries. We know very little before about real propulsion forces of October revolution and about causes of its fatal failure. Our own tragic experience helping us penetrating into real events what were happened under the carpet of Bolshevik's lieders. We have fixed and measured the gravitational waves of real politic after Big Ban of revolution, when dirty police, corruption played decisive role into creating new system and the great ideas and mottos forgotten forever.

What had been in darkness long time, now opened to our eyes in its absolute transparent and harsh nakedness.

And maybe this kind of knowledge and awareness might be helpful for avoidance or at least for diminishing despair and pains from a new circle of tragedies and calamities looming to all of us in that century.

The oldest son of Sharip and Samara Kantoro
Toktomamatov with the wife Meerim

IX

The winning and losing strategies of game theory

(inspired by Kantoro Toktomamatov, the oldest son of Sharip Jeenbekov and his dissertation and researches in cost-effective discipline and his twins that sometime casted outlook into our reality through his behave, thoughts and way of making deal with the ever changing environment).

How many problems, unsolved questions and matters have faced we are all in this world and reality! We have had only one tool and way for more or less successfully deal with - our mind and its capability to gain theoretical and practical values and knowledge. And how often it our great heritage of billions year of Evolution has suppressed, underestimated, undervalued, disrespected or even totally ignored and banned! No wonder that our world is going to the end and most religious as the our key suppressors of our mind have cultivated such self-destructive way of thinking and lifestyle.

The British mathematic John Nash had created the marvelous mathematical equation for winning strategy in card games when you have limited date and information about real situation around the table where sitting another gamers, with the cards on hands and strong desire to beat you.

I don't know exactly how looked this formula, it was probably something very difficult to understanding and imagining for ordinary mind but it's basically idea is very good and simple: we never know all dates and information in full volume as we wanted and we often made acting fast, used what we gained and know yet to reach success.

Yes, it is a brilliant principle and way of acting, because we never know perfectly what happened around us but those who acted correctly on the base of the reachable dates and information have a much better chances for victory, compare with them, who expressed negligence to accessible facts or suffered from excessiveness and perfectionism and great demand for knowledge.

But in our case if we are turning opinion for what happened in our Kyrgyzstan in politic, private and common life and traditions, we found out that we used to our own national "great invention and equation" which might be called as the successfully losing strategy in game theory. When in conditions of obscure date and information about what happened in our reality, we ever thinking, planning, dreaming and acting with the worst way for our survive and safety.

I bring here some remarkable examples for the proof of my words:

The gap between words and real deals

Despite the independent status of our state and strongly democratic and patriotic rhetoric on the every level of our society and government bodies, Kyrgyzstan has moved increasingly into opposite direction, toward a new form of slavery invented by modern Russian experts and sophisticated propaganda. Not only our president, government and predominant majority of Kyrgyz parliament wanted it and acted correspondingly but the opposition lieders and movements are drifted and pressed our society into the same direction, even wanted more strongly joining our state with Russia. As a result, we are all, our country have progressively losing independence and freedom and correspondingly our lands, strategic resurges, water and so on. Of course, such wrong and misery politic has leading unavoidable to growing poverty and weakness of our society, for the increasing various crisis's, dissatisfactions and frustrations into Kyrgyz national mentality and just into our economic environment.

Reaction of society

And what is the reaction of our society for such apocalyptic course? We are proceeding spending more and more what we still have in our property for the various traditional spendrifts', festivals, toys, and jubilees, commemorations, instead of investing this small and fast shrinking amount of resources for education of our growing generation, for real infrastructural values like good roads, communications and so on or just for really working businesses.

Advises of elders

And what kind of advices we have given from our wise elders, aksakals in such heavy circumstances?

Instead of telling the great truth and really valuable things at their last years and days as the best heritage for the next generation these old rascals have to clearly show that they much more worried about own expensive and lavish post-mortal procedures and ceremonies then about our dying freedom and independence! No one of them will want to die on the edge of saber or sharp knife to give own life for our future and freedom but all preferred rotten alive onto warm bed and after death they keep the hope for the great commemoration in their honor with the excessive gastronomic food for hundreds and thousands visitors. All our elders dreamed about the post-mortem sacrifices of two-free horses and twenty sheep and gouts as minimum and preparing foods of gargantuan sizes and volumes. That is why our general folks so loved and adored such solemn performances because they have had chance for eating the fresh meal and supper without paying for that.

Many elders are clearly understanding about fatal consequences of such massively disbursements for their children but cannot help it until they alive and after their death the Kyrgyz tradition has acted with unusually firm, certain and consistent way leading us to poverty and misery.

The killer traditions and our ecology

Such kind of Kyrgyz national competing in our society when everyone tried to be the best in massively spendrifts, leveling themselves for the most respectful and rich families, killing and eating lot of horses, cows, sheep, gouts in our multiple ceremonies, we have eaten down our forests, pastures, lands and other national treasures and could not to stop this fatal drifting. Our impact for global warming has very substantial. It would be much better for our personal welfare and prosperity of nation and country and reducing Global warming if we subtracted substantially the total number of livestock grazing in our pastures, preventing totally from entering livestock into forest area and do many other wise steps for limiting our traditional expenses, nurturing false honor and pride. John Nash firmly recommended us what we need to do in such heavy situation, what kind of socio-economical behavior actively used for, for the winning strategy. But we preferred used to the losing strategy in thoroughly and repetitively worsening situation in our local environment and in Global area.

Comparison Switzerland and Kyrgyzstan in the matter of attitude to forests

You find out entire differences between our suffered and dying forests as we have seen them today in Sary-Chelek, Arstanbap, Jeti-Oguz and other remotest regions and the dense grown and healthy jungle-like looking forests of Switzerland and Germany that coming very close to the big towns like Basel, Munich and others. They (Germans and Switzerland's) have never permitted graze livestock in that forest, these Europeans have really lived for the forest and its welfare, firmly protecting them. In sharp contrast to them we lived for our ambitions and expensive ceremonies and great love for horse meat which destroyed our environment.

About scientist in the top of state

Does the prominent Scientist able to be a good president? Of course, does it, the question of simply rhetorical, namely man of science deserved to be a good governor for the clear reason of using scientifically way of thinking, searching and finding the answer for various problems.

But Kyrgyz people had own very bad experience with the scientist on top of state, because our first president of independent Kyrgyzstan was "an modern outstanding physician and mathematic" Askar Akaev.

That is why this investigative article of Daniar Aitman of the truly scientific background of Askar Akaev so remarkable and important for rehabilitation and confidence for the people of science in Kyrgyzstan. Because our people after 15 years of shameful governing of our first president Askar Akaev since the beginning of our independence, disbelieved wholly to the science's representatives as the possible candidate for presidency.

Our people, among them especially the representatives of older generation, many told and disputed now about Akaev and his fatal presidency. Many firmly believed that he was the smartest man and a prominent scientist, which recognizes by the world, but he was a bad president and such notions badly affected and cast a black veil for the entire Scientific's community of Kyrgyz Republic. Incidentally, Kyrgyz language produced for that account the next proverb: better good shepherd than good academics come to the top power of state.

In fact, in the face of Askar Akaev instead of honest scientist and academic we had a clever con artist and scoundrels and this fact all explained and make clear - why all our reforms failed and our people so suffered at first years of our independence, when we had so many good lucks and historical great chances but all had going wrong and lost for nothing.

It a different story - the general level of Scientific's elite of Kyrgyzstan which is still remained on lower point, and upon such environment Askar Akaev looks as pretty good man of science.

Aitman gives as the very authentic picture who was Askar Akaev really and how he made his fantastic fortune in science and politic and haw he still supports own fake images and international authority.

After this totally corruptive and dishonest ruler, it is so hard now to try to learn from European, especially Switzerland, experience and traditions. Every time when we brought some references and similarities between East and West, Kyrgyzstan and Switzerland and trying to do the best, skeptics said us: "We are not Switzerland. We had once a competent and well-educated president and we know well what is going on from such experience, when we trying to do Switzerland from Kyrgyzstan. That is not way for us."

The toll it's took in our collective mind and mentality is a worst bit. Our people disbelieved to the mind and knowledge, for good education in power, preferring to choice just a strong governance and firm and even cruel ruling. And such tendency of mass thinking seems to me as a really dangerous threat for our best hopes, independence and prosperous future.

All countries worldwide need for a scientifically competent and well-educated staff in power.

I am hoping after that remarkable article our people will not more mixed with each other such utterly incompatible things as Akaev and science and Scientific's community, Akaev and Democracy, Akaev and our natural desire to create from Kyrgyzstan another Switzerland.

How to win a losing game in soul and mentality

Do not waste time for negative reaction, hatred and complaints and other such things, even if you have lived in hard situation and environment. Do their work steadily and diligently and keep attitude with the corresponding organization and people with the practical way, suggesting your best ideas and learning from them, which clearly showed the good results and strengthening your lings and helped to move ahead.

Love and respect yourself and do always the best for yourself, for growing yours competence, self-awareness, creativity and positive influence for the surrounding people for its benefits and prosperity and advance of your family.

Avoid perfectionism. Remember about winning strategy of John Nash. Absolute perfection beyond our limits and horizons but always aimed to do the best for our creativity and reputation. It is crucially important to love perfection and beauty but must not been enslaved by them.

Create and support relates, contacts with you close and far environment and traditions from that point of view and long-termed strategy. Do all what make help you and your family go ahead toward self-realization and happiness and avoid all that things, intentions and people which contradicted and destroyed those yours values.

Learn English and attached as firmly as possible to democracy's values and treasures, which make have really helped to open the great human resources hidden from us thousands years.

in Economic activities

Support spirit of creativity through establishing free market institutions and entertainment activities.

If you president do all for enfoldment this kind of energy of your people, start the big, long-termed projects and investments if such deals are leading to massively growing of local small and middle sized business activities.

in Education

Support the practical sciences and applicable knowledge's, the business schools.

in English learning

Use it or lose it. Actively using what you learned just now in the very last instance. Not keeps it in memory as things in storage, but fixing it through active use. Better used than stored and you stored and kept it much better through using.

in Politic

Not talk much about freedom but think and act as free man and head of nation. And yours people begin to awoke for freedom, for the free and better choices.

The law of Red shifting for personal application

It is quite ordinarily, understandable and essential thing, when our remembrances about our loved ones who passed, by the time will going to look up more and more dear, attractive and beautiful in our perception, mental reflection and remembrance. There is not any illusion; it is a pure manifestation of law of Red shifting.

Everyone going out wants to leave to those who left or coming into life the best legacy what he had, gained in soul and mind for his lifetime.

That's why we not only returned in our remembrances about our past time, when we were together and happy with dear ones, once more we often going further, provoking and revoking our twins from other worlds that actively participated, mixed and involved to our recalling, redesigned and recreated them and as a result have made our revealing exceptionally beautiful.

That is the law of Red Shifting, the law of beauty shifting. Of course, what we have seen in "our reality" what known as our life is only the smallest part of our real existence and life in Superposition.

The law of Red shifting for society and nation

We are all loved and deeply respected in soul the English parks, rock-music, football and generally the style of life belonged to the highest elite of UK. Why is that so? Why Albion so magnetized the lucky, famous and rich persons from East and West? The answer is simple and self-evident, because the inhabitants of this island at first found out the way to the great future through establishing the principles of open society, freedoms, which caused so many cultural, historical and human achievements – all these blazed consequences have had irresistible attraction for all nations worldwide. Instead of creating democracy and honest life in own state and soil many people with means and money preferred to escape abroad and entered to Eden created by others.

God for them, super richest oligarchs and oils magnates, sons, and daughters of dictators and toppled presidents who found out save haven in UK. We now mentioned the quite different people than these "influential figures". We told about the some sort of "migrants" who just loved West countries without strong desire and impetus to captivate them. I mean general public and wise society that more involved in the work to creating such better environment in own native land than run away abroad. They are also deeply loved West and England but expressed these senses with practical works in own soil, trying to create and recreate something alike, resemble in quite different environment. Instead to emigrate into West, they attract one by one the principles of West to native land, implanted own soul and heart by the seeds of democracy even though some of them lived long decades and even centuries on deserts of incompetent and injustice ruling.

So it's a natural phenomenon and once more those who despised such tendencies and attraction of West, looking as abnormal persons and enemies of human. Yes, sure, only those who have not knowledge and live in darkness of incompetence or those who enslaved by evil and sinister politician, oligarch or sheikhs might to despise and hide this values from generals. And lieders of Custom Union and CIS countries so involved in the matter of creating own union and democracy because abscessed with protection own people from West influences. As did it USSR in Cold War years and does it now North Korea and other dictatorships regimes.

However, truth is invincible and universal. We are all want to live in West, according with its law and principles.

And it's absolutely naturally desire and intention to be gentle, polite, peaceful citizens of honest and responsible state – we are all Englishmen in our truly depth – we are all dreamed one day expressed themselves as the Beatles, as the UK top division footballers and so on. And more our fathers and mothers in their best reincarnation or our recollections look like Winston Churchill or Queen of Great Britain. Our world want to be as UK. That is the consequence of universal law of attraction. Nobody doesn't like to be captured in wrong place and wrong time by evil person and evil state. All nations and all persons despite the great diversity of humankind have always dreamed and wanted to be as free as birds.

The Leader's mad Love

*This leader might be fatally mad and wrong
even though he looks very charismatic, brave and healthy.
Yes, he has really loved his country
and so utterly strong and intense
that will preferred suffocating entire nation to death
than push it up to the freedom.
He spate to justice, honest election, Magna Carta
and other democratic laws and hocus-pocus
of cursed Freedom and Liberty,
but he supports all Monsters and Goblins
who also despised and hated reforms,
(which may turn out the wrong course to a better side)
calling all this mental treasures and receipt of saving
as the Jewish trifles and tricks worldwide.*

*He diligently and precisely
undermined and broken all rules and moral codes
in his stagnantly fallen kingdom.*

*And after two decades
such monopolistic governing
the millions people under his ruling
still not have any rights and choices
as the base for responsible government,
they have not any choices
except to be degrading or run out abroad
or hope for afterlife or for the better environment
in other superposition.*

Loopholes into other universes

Migrants taking to get Europe used the open window of opportunities, risking sink in Mediterranean Sea, richest men and magnates from various unreformed corner of Globe paid millions to buy UK citizenship and what need to do for the simple men who lived somewhere to far from the border of Schengen area?

They attacked in dreams and fantasies UK and West Europe, hoping to reach these Promised Land and islands after another great transformation, maybe after death when they souls departed in the other world.

But I found out much better solution thank for Superposition. We need created black holes and loopholes in our reality if we cannot done the other thing for escaping from dying version of our reality. No one does not like to live in North Korea or reincarnated USSR, except maybe top lieders!

So the best thing what we can do if we were born in hell of injustice and hellish propagandistic empire that is repeat the father Sharip's choice and fate - to committed in life for the children's sake, adapted them to survive in old world and from other hand be prepared for the utterly new reality.

Of course, this man not lived into two different realities, he had not any idea about neither Superposition, neither about theory of Convergention of prominent soviet scientist, politic and dissidents Andrei Sakharov, even he very little knew about principles of West democracy and civilization, Magna Carta and so on. However, he was truly democrat by his nature because he very strong loved his children and lived for their surviving, success and future.

So we need to do the same thing if we want better future for our children. Look around carefully and you will see as many other wise person, institution and societies, created loopholes to save their best ideas and hopes.

Such project of US government in Kyrgyzstan as Independent Media support Center in Bishkek, radio-translation "Azattyk" (Freedom), UK office BBC on Kyrgyz language, the various programs of USAID in our country supporting locale business, reforms in various branches of republic and municipal government – all these ventures, technics, practices and trainings will help us created way to the more better future, even if we now lived in such reality which opposed to the West fruitful influence. Turkey universities and colleges that opened in our Kyrgyzstan – another one system, which also leaded our young generation to the West through Turkey.

American university in Kyrgyzstan, which opened in Bishkek almost 20 years ago by the initiation of Kamilla Sharshekeeva - one of the excellent loophole that lead into the bright future.

The golden mining company "Kumtor" - the loophole in economic, mining industry which clearly show to all our people the new standards of modern technologies despite the great danger to our ecology from activities of this company – all these unpleasant things happened from immerse greediness and irresponsibility's of our officials deeply involved and trapped to local and global corruption.

Our business persons like Emil Umetaliev, Tabyldy Egemberdiev also created loopholes to the future for the new generation of our entrepreneurs and managers in the tourism sphere and update services.

What happened in Ukraine in last two years and heroic fighting its citizens for democracy and joining to European civilization - one of the most impressive and great loophole which turn this country toward EU and lead out from the trap of Mordor[22].

At last but not lest we hoped for Russian democratic and pro-Wests political movement and its great influence for our region, mentality and people.

Kyrgyzstan have own democratic elite that actively fighting for the best future for our nation. Among them such persons as Nurbek Toktakunov, the lawyer that appealing to government about lawlessness many steps and procedures of entering Kyrgyzstan into Custom Union, such lieders of NGO sector as Anara Mambetova-Finkelstein, Manas Samatov, Leila Sahidbek, Ainura Cholponkulova, the ex-deputies of Kyrgyz Parliament Ravshan Djeenbekov, Omurbek Abdyrakman, journalist Naryn Ayp and many others our citizens who categorically disagree with the course of our temporal government turned out for enforcing strategic partnership with Russian Federation – they are all digging the loophole for future escaping from this trap.

Such our thinkers and philosophers as Omurbubu Begalieva, Emil Kanimetov created loophole in mental, spiritual level.

The same thing had done Sharip aba to save own children in Soviet time and I am also all my creativity turned to create loophole going out from our totalitarian reality and post-reality – as far as possible from that cursed model of governing.

The selfish gene

Selfish gene is the one of first show of conscientiousness and democracy in wild nature. Conscientiousness and democracy are equal things that is the one thing.

---

22   Mordor – the area of Death and Dark forces from Tolkien's novels.

Quantum world as the foundation of our world and Universe is kingdom and weird realm that created by Democracy in its highest level known as Superposition, where all possible and existed together – past, present and future. It's an apotheosis of Democracy.

The big man playing with universes

The world-famous mathematician Sir Roger Penrose, in fact, a great scientist.

Here's what he said, literally, in his lecture "Seeing through the Big Bang to another World"

"We have created a precise formula which allowing to see the details of big galaxies and massive black hole belonged to another universe which leaving specific marks and patterns on the outward core of our universe.

I think we will not dwell on this subject to much, those who want to, can deepening into the theory and calculate and see not only the galaxy, but the stars, planets and even living creatures on those objects - people inhabiting the neighboring universe.

In principle, this is not a difficult matter and big deal. Even if you wish you can see the every creature that lives there and understand how they communicates, make a love, and so on.

We turn to the problem of classification of universes that surround our universe, and actively interacted with - through the several cycles of eons and infinity".

To drowning island from never sinking one

Kyrgyzstan made a right decisions when four years ago canceled the visas for the visitors from developed nations of Europe, America and Asia and it step had a good consequences for our international prestige and tourism.

However, I would suggest going a little further. Western Europe, as you know, faced today with the unprecedented immigration crisis: about one million immigrants from the Middle East settled there and not have seen yet the end of this processes.

In addition to, Global warming also put own problems, some areas of Britain and other countries have seriously affected by the floods - about 10 thousand inhabitants of the north-east of England have lost their homes. Of course, this great country will easily cope with all the problems, including the effects of floods.

But I think it would be very good if Kyrgyzstan announced its readiness to host and provide land, for example, thousands of Britons who have lost their homes or live in an area where floods are inevitable.

We have a lot of vacant land in our regions and inviting the British residence to be our citizens we not only make our nations and countries close to each other but also, I am sure, contribute for economic recovery of our country. After all, why we have to hide the overwhelming tendency, this specific feature of our ancient mentality due to it the all Kyrgyz people have wanted close communication with the West, and wanted go there. Maybe it makes sense to simply invite the West to Kyrgyzstan? Right now when UK has experienced temporary difficulties and many Englishmen thought and believed that their island drowning into sea, like Titanic and actress Keith Wingslet on its board waited in wane his hero and savior! Yes, Kyrgyzstan has the excellent historical chance as that poor lad of Di Caprio for expressing himself with the best side, come up quickly to love and offered his help?

What you thing about such idea and suggestion? Let Selin Dion sing a song for us too in a future.

Kantoro and Meerim with the children and grandchildren

X

Some keen revealings from Sharip's doppelgangers

The delicate way of modern colonization

How can it be right what is been revealed in last years, thank for independent investigating and learning what had happened in our urban area, how built our city and which the priorities existed, who had privileged position and who suffered? When thousands people from Russia and other part of USSR had massively influx to our country. Invited by central government in Moscow and local communist party lieders to Kyrgyzstan, under the call for international help and support to small national country modern urban infrastructure, plans, cultural objects and convenient housing, shortly say helping Kyrgyz's to make big leap toward prosperity and happy future if Communism.

Yes, declared ideas were marvelous, but all these activities have launched with quite different way and going from first step to the last toward opposite direction. Yes, all these thousands outcomers from others part of USSR had done a great job - built modern plants, housing buildings, but all that done for themselves. Not for our people and country.

Such things very well known in history of humankind as one of the subtlest form of modern colonization, not the international help, support and expressing the friendship.

The ultimate delights of our pretty exited era

I remembered in the first year of our independence somewhere at 1995 one woman exclaimed - We have lived now in pretty exited era! – exalting by market economy, wild capitalism and its wonderful opportunities.

Of course, if you have good luck to belong to powerful environment, when yours very influential brother taken the top position among Kyrgyz governor elite, presented you for private property the whole towns market.

Really, it was a unique time in our history when robbers even did not know what they done and who they are.

-Yes, we have lived in very excited time, - exclaimed the prominent modern psychiatrist, telling about latest combined discoveries, new technologies and great advances into revealing the brain function.

-It gives us unprecedented capability to change our brain for the better. As a result we have better life, society and world, more deeper dive in the depth of nature, more far going in space and time, tend to be even in ordinary life much more foreseen, inventive, extraordinarily, much more thinking and acting efficiently and of course have been more happy, satisfied, well balanced and harmonies.

The skeleton into cupboard of Kyrgyz policy

The Northern tribalism and sectarianism which have ruled and defined the Kyrgyz policy and society in last half-century, that is our national skeleton into cupboard, which carefully hidden and camouflaged by our powerful elite and its contagious old advisers and aksalkals that could not still go out from our prehistoric nomadic era and mentality.

The Russian and Kyrgyz worlds

We have to great interest and value to the World and future as the Kyrgyz Republic, not as a part of "Russian world" in our land or one of the remnants of the dismantled USSR.

Yes, we have authentic historic, cultural value as a part of Kyrgyz world, even if this world gradually degraded and vanished. Even if Russian world defeated completely the Kyrgyz world and assimilated, our reality and historic legacy not lost his value and great interest for the Humanity.

So I turn to all our writers, scientists, experts, politicians – please, live, work and fight as a truly citizens of Kyrgyz Republic, work and create on Kyrgys and for Kyrgyz, for future not for past of Kyrgyz world. Because, we simply have not other ways for decent and really immortality and greatness except to be a worthy and great citizen of state of ancient Kyrgyz.

The main reason of our fatal weakness

When we come to such extremely vital things in our reality, like our independence, state's language, democracy, we must despised plan "B", scrap plan "B" as advised Bo Yeson. Put all eggs in one basket, get our option, watch our production and go through the roof.

Our problems and the roots of all our lacks and failings and disability to go ahead, to get a whole leg into our independence and national sovereignty have to grow from fatally lack of commitment and involvement in our freedom and historical great chance, that come once in 1000 years. Due to that negligence, lack of experience and responsibilities and obligation before history and our future generation, we gradually lost, diminishing and degrading all elements and attributes of our independence and our Kyrgyz language can not going out from vicious circle and list of endangered species.

It's our nature - to go on top position. Bo Yeason said surround you with people, who see greatness in you. You must willing destroy everything in your life that not excellent. We have to go over publicity, over average, over Kicelev's zombie-boxes, called Russian state TV and propaganda.

We have to connect and deal with the states and nations, who equivalent to our desire to be the great and best. If not - we must extricate ourselves from such kind of friends and environment. We on the side of our nature, to be the best, it is our nature to be as Singapore, Estonia, Israel, Germany, Japan.

I not having others, I hate this world of non-reformable mediocrity, the world of old rascals and rotten in limitless and uncontrolled power and corruption. Its all the way of averageness from the post- soviet comradeship.

How reshape yours past

Its look like
walking through the wild jungle
where myriads fears, doubts, hatreds and other mental evils trapped you
stiffing, browbeating and killing your energy and self-identity.

You just need for make yours soul more healthy and happy
going forward to your past experience
and replace these mental bugs, vampire and predators
inhabited yours sub-consciousness so densely
with the more friendly flora and fauna
as if that would be your past life and experience
creating environment much more kind and healthy
or reshaping these monsters and wild creatures, poison trees and other
cursed legacy
with the ever refreshing and reviving wonders of Democracy.

The policy of planned schizophrenia

Telling about USSR, we have eventually understood and concluded
that it was an epoch of progressively policy of planned hatred of
freedom, which lead unavoidable to lack of confidence, wrong doing
with the states dementia and social schizophrenia.

Doing good job even better

Sometimes very hard to live in Kyrgyzstan and stay in safe from
growing insanity (insane). The most part of people is very conservative
and holds traditions firmly, some of which outdated and clearly hostile,

that have producing so many difficulties, conflicts and clashes in our everyday existence.

Of course, some or other members of family sometimes frustrated in such environment, expressed lack of willingness for combining works, for support and keep a good relations and broadening the base of influence and common efficiency. But we have to go over such timely difficulties.

It's mean work hard and consistent even in utterly inconsistent environment, keeping tendency doing good job even better.

The unavoidable tendency

Soon or late, every woman in our world have to be look as average Englishwoman. In soul, mentality, behave and even in physical appearance. Certainly with the some national features, differences and peculiarities. The same will happened with the men. Every one of them soon or late transformed astonishingly to the common English husband with his common excellent qualities, politeness and respect to wife and truly gentleness. Not sure about the traditional English humor, maybe this gift planted in our soul not exactly well.

The explanation of such consequences is simple: as it well known widely that Englishman in family is the best husband in the world. Also very known that the best women and wives in the world – very warm, polite and ready to self-sacrifices for the benefits of family and husband - have lived in our region, among us.

But this kind of marvelous female has actively threated by globalization and many other temporarily problems and challenges – they have the status of endangered species and barely survive to the end of the century. So we have to be happy and show more respect for our dear ones, appreciating better who they were by nature and our traditions - up to now and who we are themselves. Kiss these truly miracles, unrepeated and unique in crossroad of human civilizations and epochs until them vanished at all, transforming soon to the tight, demandive and subtle mate and partner of life. Yes, all the world turning to be as England. Our state, education system, tradition and even we ourselves and our wives. Except maybe, English humor which settled and fitted not so well in our soil.

Our extra-painful problem

Even this extra-difficult and painful problem that twisted and spiraled fatally around the status and safety of our woman in family is simply resolved if we going along the right trek.

For Kyrgyzstan and entire our region, especially the fate of young wife, when she begins to live with her husband and mother-in-law under one roof and older woman sometime beginning to be very intolerable to his young "rival" and make a real threat for her – this is all the direct result of underdeveloped institutions of democracy. Just the strict obedience to the laws of the legal community can lead to a peaceful resolution - out of such conflicts between mother-in-law and daughter-in-love, and stop all kinds of violence in the family.

And ones more, it is "saved the world" not only in the cases when husband mocked his wife physically and mentally effecting her often under the support of his mother and national traditions, but when the head of a family or mother-in-law in old age going to be helpless and weak – in the same time when grown and matured daughter-in-love turning gradually into a tyrant herself for vindictive punishing old woman for the past humiliations and entering into own rights and respect for ruling by the new generation of brides, wives of her own children.

To stop this vicious circle and never-ending nightmare, there is no other means and ways than to develop democratic institutions in the family, on the state level and entire society and supporting education, especially among female. No other ideology or religion does not know better a way out of this fatally twisted and spiraled tangle of family contradictions.

We are all so poor, contagious and vindictive because do not know and recognize the painful but blessed rights of others neither we know own rights and obligations.

Out of curiosity

It seems our top rulers and first presidents just out of curiosity have accepted the warmly invitation to the West and Democracy. However, when comes time for deal and real reforms on the way to European values, they had to show their truly mundane, mediocre and awful nature, grabbled by insatiable greediness, total corruptions and fatal weakness that turning to massively treachery of our national interest, priorities and independence.

xxx

Never look to the one point as for the fixed anchor. Stick to the panoramic piece of view, look to the moving and confining square and other shapes and figures and volumes which contained what interested you. Better imagine these various shapes and squares as flying, swimming or better dancing objects which bearing something very useful for you. Our vision is the Quantum phenomena and miracle, as the all things surrounding us.

We could keep them in better shape in their primarily beauty and wonder only if we submit ourselves the Quantum rules and laws of that great and mysterious game.

How to learn English?

Turn attention not to the separate words but for the whole part of sentence, even more to the content of paragraph and a dialogs. Focusing your attention to the word's combination, to the natural speech patterns, which have used by native English speakers

Play with English words, sentence and English speakers, English cultural values, with the best and worst side of their mentality, with the quick and sharp British humor – do such things as often as possible, playing with English dialogs, Magna Carta, Democracy, Human rights, space program, Quantum Physic and so on with the best worlds advances.

Why we so hated Gorbachev?

Its naturally for slaves to hate lieder who gave them freedom. It needs lot of time until majority will get what did this man and be thankful to him. In the other hand the majority has predisposed to adore the strong men and dictators even if they stole its freedom and presented slavery and killed most of them. They loved dictators for their cruelties and a lot of time passed until they felt bad and shocked from such kind of love.

Even the free nations sometimes will dream about own "strong guy" and lot of people despised and hated the truly democratic lieders like Barak Obama.

How stop to hate and afraid people and things which seems unpleasant, undesirable or even fearful for you when you walking outside

Myopia is the complex dysfunctional pathology of human eyes, mind and body which gradually rump up as the result of abnormal behavior and disharmonized intentions. Short seeing born as parasites from tinniest eggs and developed on our bad habits, false traditions or misconceptions.

One of the main of them is belief that many people around you, that familiar or not with you predisposed dislike and even humiliate you.

You just not want to look to them, you hide your eyes, intentionally cut out their sharpness and turning them inside, when you going outside. As a result of such abnormal and stupid behavior, your vision capability failed down.

So what need to do to reverse this process and returning again to normal and healthy seeing?

First of all, keep relaxing, when you walking outside, no one look for you and planning against something awful. All people around you busy with own problem, and if the sometimes turned to you with not very pleasant way it is just yours imagination.

Look pleasantly and friendly around - to all people and others objects that meet you, which surrounding you. Let your eyes freely and happily communicate with them, investigate them, danced with them.

Look as far as possible when you deal with some or other man, especially if someone really dislike you, not avoid him, not focusing to his weakness, mistakes and miseries and imperfectness. Training your eyes in body and soul look, find and investigate the hidden tendencies and treasured intentions and beauties in his nature and soul and tune your perception and mood to communicate and deal with the best part of every human that met you.

If you step to this road and mental attitude and not turning back you soon getting to heal yourself and find out as good vision starts to return you.

When you left alone

Do the same things with your dreams, fantasy and thoughts, when you staying along. Fears, worries and other badly controlled emotions are also influenced very destructively to our body and soul health and going to slow down of our vision capabilities.

If bad things, suppositions and nightmares haunted you stubbornly and sticky and you cannot just a switch off them, jump to their company, communicate bravely with all these creatures from your inner universe, not afraid and avoided them, but keep balance, harmony and courage.

Never look to one point, but get observation as broader as possible. Absolutely all mems and remembrances and reflection of your past experience overburdened with your temporal influences and emotion, which look so dysfunctional, fretful and disheartening for you - all of that is just a one dimensional outlook and reflection of your life which in reality much more rich, bigger and differently. It's true, we are living among monsters, thank for our distorted vision.

In reality, all these things much more complicated, vibrant and constantly changeable and reformative.

So look broader and you not only better understand and appreciated the world around you and inside you, but also coming up to road leading to the more harmonious world with much better precise and sharp focusing them.

The reformatted past and soul

He returned to early stage of his memories to find and hook out all negative senses, experiences and impressions for replace them with the good and happy remembrances and counterparts, often artificially designed and implanted in the bottom of soul.

The icebergs of outdated traditions

Break down and melt these massive icebergs of prejudices and outdated traditions in your mentality and soul, which hold up all your natural reserves, forces and energies. These dirty and poisonous glaciers 1000 years kept tightly the living water of freedom, happiness and prosperity.

The Black Holes of opportunities

The modern technologies, sciences and reforming human being and culture are going to be so advanced, acute and attractive, inspiring and marvelous that everyone who trying to dig deeply risked lost themselves forever after the next step and turn on the road of this strangely and fast transformed reality.

It may have to confirm as a matter of fact, that the Black Hole of fantastic opportunities and immeasurable discoveries waiting for you greedily everywhere and every instant - whatever we are trying to do or planned, after making the first step we often involved and captured by the great force of suddenly unfolding secrets of nature.

The double autopilot technology of praying and learning simultaneously for reaching multiple blesses and effects

The autopilot technology of doing simultaneously multiple deals and duties together with the creating namaz - that is the most efficient way and technology for increasing productivity when various ideas, sentences, suggestions and resolutions outflowing themselves and abundantly, that is a truly system and mental exercise for the exceptionally fast reaching to unavoidable success in your life.

Praying or meditation or inspiration is the key factor for gaining success. However, of course many things depend from the power of your mental exercise and repetition, its duration, from yours personal sincerity and diligence when you turn to the Heaven.

But god or evolution or somebody also like immeasurable advanced alien has a very strange sense of humor, he created people undoubtedly from monkey and lead them mercilessly from so many tests and sufferings, eventually producing such marvelous creature as we are.

We must know firmly, before turning to him, that we have deal with the scientist who waited from us the real results, achievements and progress. So maybe our passive praying not liked him much and he preferred more active, zeal and vivid steps and intentions from us?

That's why I am warmly recommending you my technology of combined spiritual activities like praying to Christ, creating namaz toward Mecca, Buddist meditation to nothing, Hinduisms worshipping of cow, Tengrian adore to nature or dedicating to Quantum Physic and other such innumerous believes and exercising – its depend from your personal choices and involvement - with the concrete business, undertaking or just a work, for example learning English or washing dishes, cleaning room, lining up and systemizing your valuable papers, remembrances and so on.

If you joined namaz with the learning English or China or any other foreign language, you will immediately blessed with the substantial progress in your learning. I recommend you when you creating 5 times namaz, spending 10 minutes for every one of them, read suras from Koran on English and with the English additional turnings and inspirations and revelations. If you have done it constantly, especially if you trying digging as deep as possible, I firmly believe your knowledge of Holy book and English will be dramatically growing.

If you seriously turn to that initiation, you will granted and blessed with double and even multiple ways. Prophet asked people for praying but he also mentioned that a work is the same praying. If you well praying or well working then you reward will exponentially growing and such way and system of activities deeply marked in your mindset.

And think about what happened with you if you starting to join praying with the working and practiced do that better and better? Of course, your rewards begin to grow exponentially.

When you made the big progress and well trained in such double namaz-working strategies, you may father increase you practice in depth and broad, using extrasensory systems, self-hypnosis and art of duplication and replications and multiplications your effects and results.

Eventually you will reached such condition and perfection in yours work when every sell of your body will create namas, communicating very fruitfully with the highest intellect and enriched grandly and simultaneously with the most efficient way of learning foreign language. And of course you will bless personally for such smart and diligence belief and sagacity.

The lieders with "great love" to own countries

The Nazi lieder was originated in quite different environment, compare with phenomenon of Stalin. Adolf Hitler was born in the center of Europe, inhabited by the nation that worked and lived with the great scale of precision, foreseen and diligence and this people are learned carefully planning it's everyday's life and future - It was a perfect world and country, excellent working system, like German'roads and manufactures which produced the brilliants clocks, optical equipment's and others technological wonders. The German future also remained the perfectly designed wonderful destiny and mission.

But Hitler was a genius of evil propaganda, attracted German race with the own fantasies and cruel intentions, that were carefully implanted in German mentality and poisoned it with own vision and interpretation of future and dangerous illusions that lead all world to so fatal consequences.

He loved the great Germany more than German nation, like the national lieder of modern Russia, that loved also more Great Russia than Russian nation, but Russian people fell in deadly love to his lieder. All the bad genius did the same things - they loved the greatness and play trick with our slavish fragile conscience and sub-conscience, leading us to the hell.

Internet and dogfights under carpet

Why does Russia so hate internet that more than half of its population will be totally agree if the state authorities will cut off entire country from Web and even more do the same thing into post-soviet area?

Because its politics still adored dogfights under carpet and don't know other way of making big deals.

xxx

All our temporary problems and difficulties with the children, that growing so impulsive and unpredictable means nothing compare with unprecedented cruelty of fate, which lied down on the shoulders of our old generations. Our fathers and old brothers, uncles also were been very young and unpracticed and emotionally unbalanced, when they been sent to the battlefield of the most cruel and bloodiest war in worlds history. They were sent not to study into Bishkek or Moscow, not to the Soviet Army for make a military service, not to the far corner of great country, somewhere to Siberia for works on logging or in mining site – but right to the WWII to die on the front, when you so young, green, without any experience. And just imaging what felt mothers, wives, sisters who missed them forever.

This war was a direct result of two evil powers those cannot existed without violence and expansion. Namely, Germany and USSR together as ultimate allies and rivals of cruelties behind closing door curved up the European map and finally they attacked each other, plunging the world into a terrible massacre.

A sketchy picture from a meeting of Kyrgyz oppositions groups and leaders that just as up to neck in corruption as our rulers so eagerly competing for being grabbled by Kremlin

…One opposition group disputed about other, which proclaimed more radical announcement and openly demanded the resignation of president of Kyrgyzstan Atambaev. Some informed members said about freaking reaction of president, who promised to influential person in Kremlin that he will distributed Kalashnikov among own supporters and in any case stopped plot and killed all lieders. But other informed person said that this action of an opposition group is just the bullying game of Kremlin to make the president of Kyrgyzstan more obedient in the matter of derailing the project of China for creating Silk Road passage for train through Kyrgyzstan, which lingering China and West Europe and helped out state to find out own way for world market.

All sides have firmly agreed that such advance of rivaling opposition group has not any chance for success. Kremlin experts and policy makers just a little played with the Atambaev and after his fast visit to Moscow and kowtow to Putin and promises end up any relations with the China, our president return to Kyrgyzstan as winner and crashed completely any opposition movement. All sides have perfectly informed that Moscow is holding in its hand so vast number of keys to our state, so tightly controlled our government and opposition, that they ready to play any symphony in our political area and often just enjoyed experimenting with us as the very nice Guiney pigs. Moreover, all opposition lieders and social person in Kyrgyzstan not only perfectly understood this game but trying to play own game according with mightiest will and omniscient influence and presence of god-like Putin.

What a dismal prospect for the Kyrgyzstan and this newest highly precarious world of total dependence all our elites from Kremlin, when it lieder has took on all option of our freedom!

Shame on our opposition and rulers!

The tragic story about dying Freedom

The story about daughter that run to the fest but reach to the most tragic event in life - the loss of her mother remained me what was happened with our independence in that 25 year.

Yes, our state is the same Girl and our independence – her unhappy Mother.

We not loved and appreciated her to much; we are counted that she come to us without our strong hope, willingness and fighting for her. She just presented to us accidentally and that's why we not honored and respect her as did that others nations and post-soviet countries like Estonia, Latvia, Georgia, Ukraine.

When these countries have very strong valued and loved independence and hard work in the emerging window of new and great opportunities of history, we instead lamented about our past Soviet times when we had not our Independence and any opportunities at all. Of course we was a part of USSR, the great military empire and many of us proud with that fact and even counted that it was a very fine epoch - we were all lived friendly and happily, drank chead vodka and bad beers and eat bad sausages.

And under such nostalgia we not observed as step by step going to lost our Independence. Kyrgyzstan has died in front of our eyes when we instead of joining and sticking to Europe and US and other free countries, who worshiped the principles of Freedom, we avoided them in favor of our non-free past and enslaved existence in the frame of died USSR. We not lived in freedom like free nation, we lived us enslaved post-soviet creature, we expelled US air-base from our territory, which had been one of the luckiest event in our history and downgraded systematically our relation with West in the honor of our good relation with the Russian Federation, eventually entering to the Custom Union of non-free countries.

Many people not agree with me? They counted that Kyrgyzstan must be free joining with Russian Federation. That is the same hopes that entertained girl when he run to her happy past. Of course Kyrgyzstan so strongly desired to the past fest and peace, when we drank cheap vodka in abundance and eat bad sausages, that turns out from Independence - from her old and sick mother which returned to us for the last time - and lost her forever. Instead of great historical fest and victory we come to the solemn obituary procedures of our died Freedom.

Congratulation all of us, dear kyrgyzstanian, we are lost our freedom and hopes for future!

You thought we come to peace, find prosperity and friendship to turn to our past - run to Custom Union with the Russian - as Estonia and other free and wise nations run toward European Union? You thought we are also created the happy and prosperity environment and worked for peace and prosperity worldwide? What is the nonsense and fatal miscalculation!

Yes, we fast going to total lost our freedom and peace and prosperity and more - we make a choice to live and work for the war, chaos and instabilities – local and worldwide.

Because the nature of free and enslaved nations are quite different and those who not loved freedom could not to love the West and vice-versa, who was born in prison, will feel uncomfortable in freedom and attracted again and again to prison and loved and expressed nostalgia for the dying empire.

Two kind of puppets theatre

To be a puppet in hand of West much more better, respectful and deserving to call a honest and great politic compare with deadly dancing in the hand of such lieders as Putin and Assad and legion other enemies of freedom.

The puppet of Democracy is a very good dancer.

The puppet of Dictatorship - what kind of poor, tragic and misery dancer is!

Ivan the Terrible and Teit Khan

Authoritarianism as the desire of absolute power upon country and society is the tragic disease, which needs as soon as possible for compulsory treatment and therapy.

For those who doubt, I have to recalling here the two examples from history.

Russian Tsar Ivan the Terrible had killed his son and sole heir of empire. And this event putting him in a tragic position, as well as entire Russia which lost the future king. We do not know what the qualities had the heir for more detailed speculation about his possible political future.

Compare with the Ivan Grozny the story of the Kyrgyz Teit Khan, who lived 200 years before Russian tsar, looks even more tragic and cruel from the point of historical consequences.

Teit khan allowed Jungars warrior to kill his son, the sole heir that already become the savior of the Kyrgyz nation, Kurmanbek Batyr, who defeated Jungars and Kalmyks.

Teit khan, as we know, did not give to his son his own steed, when Kurmanbek asked for it preparing for the match with the best warrior from opposite side. As a result, Kyrgyz hero was fatally injured during this risky game, because the horse, on which he rode, was not consistent with the "level of competition."

During the jump across the ravine, and the battle in the air his horse stumbled for an instance, when landed to opposite edge but it was enough: Kurmanbek could not escape from the sword of enemy, who struck him in the spine behind.

Teit Khan had been well informed about such outcome of this battle. He loved his great son, and he knew that without Kurmanbek his country doomed to perish and bitterly veiled upon his death as Ivan the Terrible, but they both loved the power much more. For sacrificing sons and the country as well. If Ivan the Terrible killed son in the outburst of badly controlled hatred when they left alone in the king's castle, Teit chan helped to Jungar's warrior to defeat his son into ancient sporting entertainment – during very risky battle on warhorses using swords, spears, daggers, maces, and other killer stuff.

The wonderful Multiverse

Hey, the theory of Multiverse gives us the enormous hope for our life. Yes, really if we are all existing in so many realities and having such many opportunities, why on earth we must worrying and trying to do something extraordinary here - in our poor reality and existence? Does the dear Superposition make the best service for all of us beforehand, since the beginning, suggesting all best options for every one, doesn't that? It's just impossible to be a loser in such kind and nice cosmically environment. Not only presidency for our Kyrgyz Republic but great number other wonderful and fantastic possibilities waited for you and me. Just imagine yourself as if being somebody like North Korean dictator Kim Chen Yn but on the top of US and senators applauded you so vividly and all America worshiped you as the Holy Grail. The great actress Sharon Stone also among them. That would be marvelous picture, wouldn't that? Or imagine yourself as the national lieder of Great Britain and Queen invited you to her golden chariot and dear London greeted you and Queen. And Kate Winslet and so many others beautiful girls cried about you. Or maybe you preferred to be somebody like the modern captain of West, Alexander the Great or better Tamerlane the Great who come to Europe and West from Central Asia and saved them from malignant and wicked Putin, the greedy oils sheikhs, religious bigotry and other kind barbaric brotherhoods – beat all of them and put into mobile prison hanging behind your golden chariot - and all liberated Mankind applauds you and make the great step ahead.

Or imagine yourself somebody like the good Terminator-Arnold Schwarzenegger who come to Earth from far future and saved our world from bad guys. All great options ready for you and me in such or other parallel realities.

So let go to drink vodka and dream about our wonderful Multiverse where in any cause you and me will be granted enormously and unavoidable. Believe me you never run out from marvelous Kate Winslet if you born in such Multiverse.

XXX

There are have all moral and legitimate reasons to hate and judge all persons, teachings and ideologies, which denied democracy. Because she is alone who does not denied anyone, any doctrine and religion, actively creating conditions for diversity, freedom and for survival all.

The formula of unite harmony in Superposition

What you thing about people wanting to know what atom do when we not looking at it? It making service for the other who did it.

And what atom did a heck a long time when human or any other kind of observers existed at all?

Some scientists believed that atoms and electrons have some sort of conscientiousness and reason because they so respondent for our mind and observation. They said about primarily, primitive form of conscientiousness, something like reaction of algae, microbes of vegetables for our outward influence for them. But due to the very quick and miraculous service of atoms and electrons and their reaction and ability to jump to past and changed them according with our hope and demand, me might say vice-versa about evidently high, paramount and amazing form of intelligence. Of course atom and electron much wiser than those humans who looking and hunting for them.

Atoms and electrons are multiverse object and that very vibrant and energetic staff applying multiverse nature of all big object around – humans, stars, galaxies - everything

That is why physics called them the parallel universes theory rather than the parallel theory of electrons, because we ourselves are made of atoms and electrons after all.

Our discoveries and increasing knowledge have a great impact to our past. Not changed them maybe but changed our attitude and perception of it.

Quantum Mechanic provided just such feedback behind. It does allowing the backwards in time, change the past to fix it up so that we can be sure we exist. So we have an influence on the past through active measurement. Increasing our knowledge and make a discoveries.

This fact is clearly witnessed about multiversal nature of our reality and it's strong relation between our past, present and future as a one close entangled whole.

Our main task – to curve, find out, calculate the ultimate formula of Multiversal harmony and nature of Superposition as it is, as it was and wanted supposedly to be a realized at future and eternity.

If we do that, we better understand what our Universe, Multiverse or Superposition really is and what it do with us, when we look to it and what it do when we don't and what wanted from us at all.

The power of knowledge

All possible if you have had the perfect knowledge and able to learn your people use this tool, mean, weapon, and act inclusively.

Kyrgyzstan primarily was, is and will be the country of kings and emperors, as the eternal cradle of great dynasties.

When every one of us find out own perfect twin and works and lives with him, we are all together created unimaginable marvel and even maybe saved to this suffered world.

Just imagine as one morning our 6 million citizens have awoken and suddenly feeling themselves as perfect and authentic heroes, stars, kings, queens and emperors, but as if they have been stripped from powers and properties, going to start their lives again on the new and unknown ground, look like rescued after a shipwreck and find themselves on a completely new land.

What will happened with our Kyrgyzstan in the case of such magical and mass transformation of our mentality and entire population from zero to hero? If instead of our president, we have seen somebody like Pericles, Mannerheim, Lincoln or Vatslav Havel? If for the states communication and IT-sectors have appointed and answered really great and innovative persons like Mark Zuckerberg, Bill Gates? If such masters as Marshall, Eisenhower suddenly starts to work for recovery and rehabilitation of our junks status economy, and our state – all its activities, businesses, undertakings in government, parliament, court system, media, music, art, theatres will getting to flourishing state, going with the same road, trek and marvel of democracy and freedoms as it happened in UK after Magna Carta, after queen Elizabeth, after William Shakespeare, after declaration of independence and freedom of US, after Churchill, Beatles and so on? Just imagine what will happened, if all your environment, close relatives and friends transformed to Fidel Castro, Tamerlan, Salman Rushdie, Sharon Stones, Nelson Mandela, Bibisara Beisheralieva, Donald Trump, Ayatollah Khomeini, Richard Gear, Lech Valensa and so on and on.

Of course, such extremely powerful society very soon will rise above Ala-Too and rapidly created with explosive way the completely new and unique environment and Kyrgyzstan. Something like Atlántida which will ready pulling out from lethargic sleeping entire Central Asia and revive and refresh completely itself as the ancient country of heavenly mountains and thousands peaks. Of course, Kyrgyzstan fast transformed to new superpower and starting to help to West and East, North, and South.

What is the hell going on into Syria? Why, sons of beaches, pro-western coalition separately from Russia and Iran participated in war? And why still not stopped conflict in east of Ukraine? What are doing, mister national lieder? Shut down and get away from such under carpet police. Get out from Donbas, Donetsk and elsewhere!

We certainly helped China make a deal with another China, called Taipei and helped India to create the good attitude with the Pakistan and Bangladesh. Moreover, we help to create a free Iran, Arabia, Afghanistan and helped many other nations and states. We stopped any kind of bigotry, dictatorship, wars – on Earth, underwater, on air, in space, hybrid's conflicts and so on, banned worldview any repressions and it's repercussions. We left for the humankind only love, friendship and greatness and we saved West Europe from global warming and sinking and from uncontrolled global migration.

The idolatry of freedom

Among the great number of ancient and modern fanaticisms and idolatries there is existed only one of them which not only permissible, but indispensable for our surviving. That is the democracy, obsession to it. Because this idolatry has really worked and helped to create this world for better place - this commitment to democracy, freedom and

Western values and nothing more. Maybe it is the Holy Grail, the highest and ultimate truth?

In fact, what could be better, honest and holy than this subtle science, beautiful set of laws that teaching us to respect and value human rights, preparing us for tolerance and planting deeply into our sole the ideas of independence, respect and evaluate of every life and freedom?

No one religion, ideology and science have to do anything like this. And the fact that almost all American presidents and the leaders of free world so devotedly praised democracy and the great achievements of these countries themselves have made the best endorsement of this truth and clearly show to us what need to be done and how – with such level of passion and purity we must involving and committing into democracy if we really want through sparkling and igniting these ideas, going to hard work and make our life to the better place for living.

The law of 100 monkeys

If the knowledge, which we gained, has a vital power for our surviving, it is going to jump up to the fastest trek - for distribution with the explosive way.

That is the tipping point from which the law of 100 monkeys going to work. When a some valuable habit, for example washing fruits and roots in water before eating them, after learning and actively using by 100 species, this process reached to the tipping point - and this habit distributed among all animals (monkey, belonging to the same group of primates) explosively. As far as human belonged to primates, therefore our society also has yielded to this law.

However, thanks for complexity of our species this rule acted differently. Just a good habits, merely wise thoughts, which not belonged to the class of extra valuable revelations not aired in time the same wake up calling, haven't chance for such superconductivity, influence and effect, they all distributed gradually among the people, at first gained by advanced layers and then gradually accumulating by general population, gaining power and weight.

The democracy principles have long time belonged to that group of very valuable and desirous things in our life but Humanity too long underestimated them, not granted and understood truth and justice hoping more for other kind extremely values for our surviving.

Now in the winter of our discontent and close up to total destruction of our civilization the democracy come up to such level of extra-meaningfulness.

That is the crucial point of our global conscientiousness. We have to as fast as possible to grasp and comprehend, receive these values if we want to survive as human. If 100 persons in every country clearly in deep level understood and appreciated this truth, then it jump up to the level of our collective mindset where igniting superconductivity and laws of 100 monkey go to work and instantly all the people owed the great truth and power of Democracy, which along make to save us from our own barbarity, hate and evilness inherited by our animals, Darwinians long-termed pre-history.

Turn again to analogy from wildlife, of course, the washing fruits and roots in water of spring, before eating them, it is good and healthy habit for surviving the monkey's society and sometime maybe even to be a crucially valuable, that is why the law of 100 monkeys is worked.

But in nature has existed another more deep rested level of communication for the instantly ongoing the critically important, extremely valuable signals which quickly and strongly defined the common social behave of wild animals, which activated in the moments of natural calamities like massively fire in forest, strong earthquakes, landslides, an asteroid colliding to planet and so on, when something extraordinary and utterly unthinkable evoked in the soul all animals, they are all transformed to close friends and relatives, totally forgiving about fight, competitions, violence, having sex, when wolves run from fire together with rabbits and foxes and tigers neck to neck with the antelopes and oxes, sometime warmly helping to each other's.

In such extremely critical instants all wild and domestic animal have got to be a truly democrats of highest level, because they clearly understand, thanks for mentioned deep signals, that only democracy might to save them, which is a first rate valuable things for collectively surviving.

However, what happen with the human being? Why we not run out with the same collectively wisdom from fire? We, who lived more than half of century, in such extremely dangerous situation and environment, when for total destruction and global calamity, left five minute? Why our species not expressed such kind of solidarity and common sense, which well-known and learned in wildlife? Maybe we still have not 100 advanced animals who clearly have seen what happened with our planet and got it to the truth, that only Democracy as the science of tolerance and collectively surviving make save us?

When in every country worldwide have emerged these 100 monkeys – I thought entire world very fast come to stop moving to the abyss and turn to peace and prosperity.

So I am turning to the citizens of Kyrgyz Republic, in searching these 100 monkeys, do you really don't believe for the upcoming last days and global calamities when we all have seen so many signs and predicaments around in local and global levels? Do you really hoping avoided wars, repressions, tortures and other testings' of last days? Do you not understand, dear friends, that we are have only one chance and way to stand for against looming Doomsday, if we stand strongly with all heart, soul and head for Democracy values and principles, which holding the West civilization?

Please, its wake up calling, maybe a last sounding, awake as soon as possible 100 Kyrgyz monkeys, if we do it, we save our children and future. We will create the Democratic state in Central Asia or neither all are going to extinction and assimilation and repressions and ethical cleansing and so on will get other rapes and fruits of violence.

But if we succeed, we saved not only themselves but also helped save entire Central Asia and our World. Because our land, Ala-Too is the cradle of kings and emperors and storage of clean water for all Asia, which played the crucial role in the matter of preventing Global warming and mass extinction.

Yes, really Kyrgyz democracy has saved entire world. Please, awake 100 monkeys worldwide!

How does it happen – the great leap forward

99% of energy and masses, that existed in Universe has remained unknown, unmeasured and wholly unused, which modern physics called as Dark Energy and Dark Matter. But they are really worked and shaped our reality and our conscientiousness, mentality, history, culture.

That's why when man and society don't knows about this great resources, they used only 1% of their hopes and energies, living in poverty and misery.

The magic clue, which help to open door leading to this great storage of this fantastic recourses we find out into our sub conscientiousness, if we learned used it with right way through training and practice for changing (or reformatting) our Superposition.

We have to follow and create only the Best in our life and imagination, extricate wholly all negative and destructive things in our mind and environment. Only through this way we have to rule and manage by our mind, body, by the myriads of well-structured atoms and electrons, jumping and dancing and living instantly here in everywhere when we looked to them and when not looking at all - and Superposition will worked and hooked subconsciously for the day by night working for your best, and Dark Energy and Dark masses will be harnessed for your benefits and achievements, manifesting marvelous things into your reality.

When 100 persons have to learned do that with right way and scientifically exactitudes, using Dark Energy and Dark Matter – their combined powers exploded and going through the roof – and suddenly thousands and 100 thousands other people in one instance jumped to understanding the great truth, which so long was sealed for them. Then society rapidly changed for better side, make a quantum leap into the great new reality.

Here is the answer and the solution of enigma about 100 monkeys.

To all countries and peoples, who believed to Democracy

I have to turn to all west world and all people, who shared and believed to Democracy. Sorry for my disturbing your peace and comfort, but our harsh and merciless and unforgivable reality made me tell and act with very pragmatic and straight way.

Everyone on Earth, who shared and believed to Democracy, please, if you able to respect Kyrgyz nation and learn its native language, you may arrive to Ala-Too for save the endangered nation of Central Asia and Democracy.

If you are all come here we are together revived and recreated the island of Democracy and more - from here erected and established the world's great empire of Democracy, which implemented and supported peace and prosperity everywhere!

Democracy is the irreducible part of highest intellect and universal conscientiousness. There are only two options in this binary reality and you might to get with justice or acted against it.

So make a choice in favor of great empire of Eurasian Democracy – right here, in the center of Supercontinent. You may have lived everywhere - in East, West, South or North, you may to be a citizens of Democratic state, or authoritarian regime or even born and grown in the ruthless and cruelest prison of totalitarian rule, - in any case, if you will fight for better future, peace and democracy, come to Kyrgyzstan and attach your soul, heart and life close to that vital country, which dreamed and pregnant with Democracy.

Give your life, hopes to Ala-Too, if you have not chance to be personal involved to that deal, give your children and dedicate your future, sons and daughters to our country.

If you not able to give yourself presently to us, attaching too strong to own prosperity, welfare and peace, give us yours better transcendences and dedicated them to Kyrgyz Republic. You have had the great number of yours twins in Superposition – send the best of them to Central Asia with the deep and great love and respect to the eternal light of truly greatness, justice and aikolduk[23].

---

[23] Aikolduk – the heavenly generosity, belonged to the greatest Kyrgyz hero and savior Manas, often this word used together with the his name as Aikol-Manas, meaning Manas the Heavenly generous.

Publications

- 1993, "Eleanor Rigby", the love story from the epoch of Cold War, (Kyrgyz and Russian version), Osh regional states print house;
- 1998, "The comet of Galley", the science-fictional story about trip to the future of Kyrgyz small village, the print house of Vera Nurgazy, Bishkek;
- 1998, "Argasyz Biznes", (Business for surviving old communist's rascals), satirical fictional play, Osh regional print house;
- 1999, "Nebesniy Kosar", (The heavenly Mover), selected verses, Russian, the private printing house of Vera Nurgazy, Bishkek;
- 2007, "Mart Ynkylaby" (The March Revolution), political-fantastical-satirical play, The print office of "Freedom house", Bishkek; http://www.epubbud.com/book.php?g=RAAXPRZ2
- 2008, «Биз –миллион эрбиз», the science of getting victory for Kyrgyz nation and state; http://www.epubbud.com/book.php?g=FRB9KDGJ
- 2011, "300 Spartanians of Osh tragic events', political tragedy, Russian, "Freedom house", Bishkek, http://www.epubbud.com/book.php?g=L88UFU5Y

- 2011, Selected political and philosophical shorts stories (The rodents of history, The talks on the slope of green hill, The modern faire-tales and others), on the site of Russian national server; http://www.proza.ru/avtor/zamir1
- 2012, Selected lyric on the site of Russian national server of modern poetry; http://www.stihi.ru/avtor/zamir1
- 2013, "Kumtordun Kyl kopurosu" (The golden Gate of Kumtor), satirical play, "Freedom house"; http://www.epubbud.com/read.php?g=LYJ39VVE&p=0
- 2014, "Eleanor Rigby", Partridge Singapore;
- 2015, "Eleanor Rigby II", Partridge Singapore;
- 2015, "The origin of ancient Kyrgyz tribes", Partridge Singapore;
- 2016, "The golden eagle of father Sharip, called Superposition", Partridge Singapore;

Achievements

- 1985, (August), The Winner of the republic competition "Young Fiction writers of Kyrgyzstan", Bishkek;
- 1996, (May), Participant of the Conference on Protection of men' rights in Europe, Prague;
- 1997, (July), Participant of the first World festival of journalists. Yalta, Ukraine;
- 2002, (September), Nominalist of the prize "Baatyr Jurnalist" (The brave journalist) given by civic community of Aksy regions, for masterpiece reflection of Aksy tragedy on March 17, 2002;
- 2004, (August) Silver Medal for the best article on ecology given by Independent Ecological Expertise on republic; competition.
- 2005, (November) Participant of seminar for journalists working in critical situations. Moscow, Russia;

- 2006-2009, with a member of official delegation of Kyrgyz Republics government visited to Japan, China, Belorus, Russia, Turkey. Met with prime ministers, presidents and others high officials of these countries;
- 2014 -2015 winner of republic competition among journalist and writers dedicated to the honor of Absamat Masaliev, nominated by Russian largest literary site proza.ru for the title of "The best writer of year".

Printed in the United States
By Bookmasters